How Not to Sell

A Sales Survival Guide

How Not to Sell

A Sales Survival Guide

by Rashad Daoudi

atmosphere press

Contents

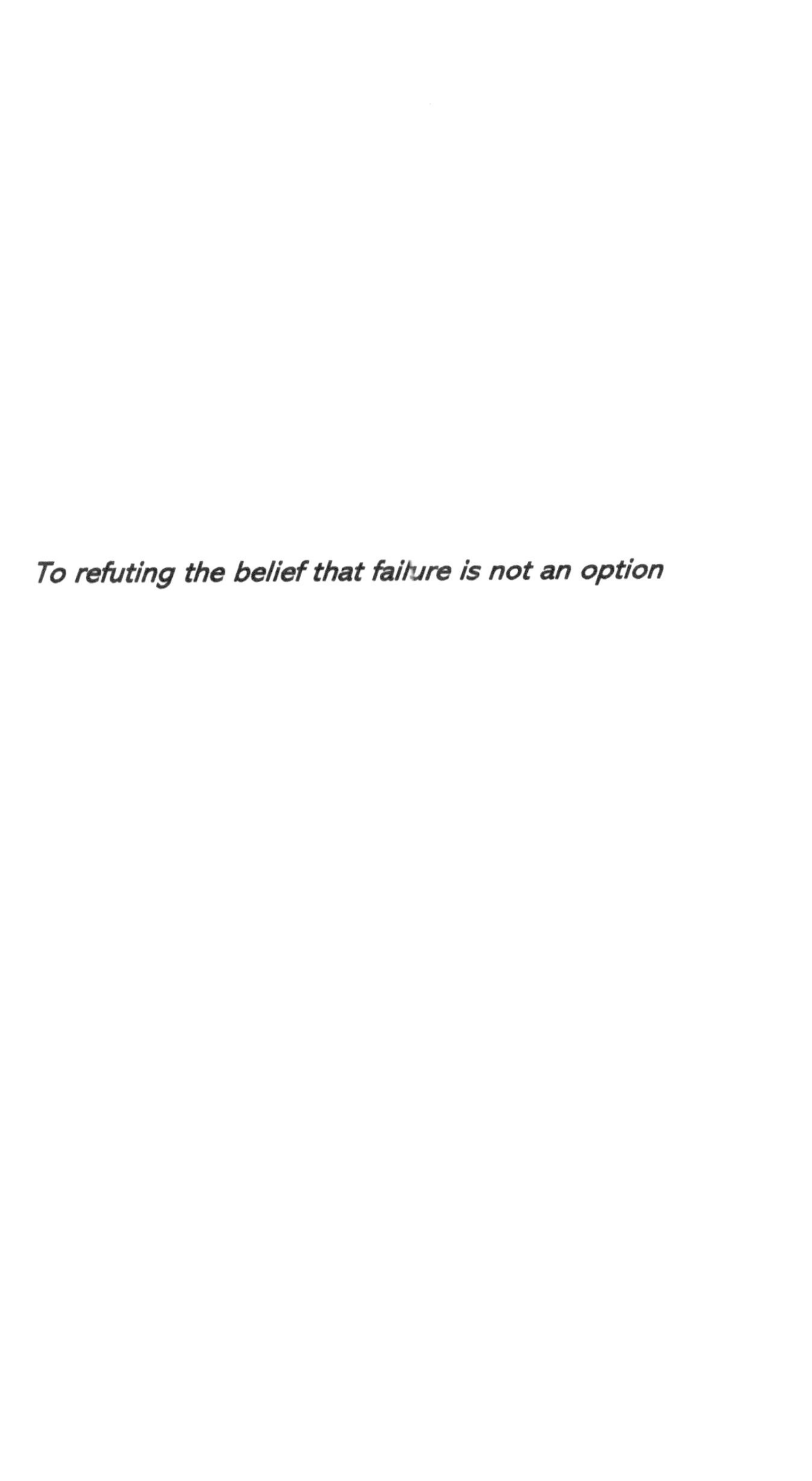

To refuting the belief that failure is not an option

Preface

*It's fine to celebrate success but it is more important
to heed the lessons of failure.*

-Bill Gates

In 2016, I came across a podcast that talked about
"survivorship bias." This concept explains why people
prefer to look at those who have succeeded as a model of
how to do it themselves. If someone wants to start a
business, it's natural they would study and implement
what other successful business owners have done.

The podcast went on to tell a story. During WWII, the U.S.
Navy was deciding where to put more armor on planes
that went on bombing runs. They could only add so much
or else the planes would be too heavy to fly. In deciding
where to put the extra armor, the inclination was to put it
where the returning planes had been shot. But then
someone suggested the eventual solution, which was to
find the planes that didn't make it back and put the armor
where they had been shot. By learning from those that
died, everyone else had a better chance of surviving.

Then it struck me. If salespeople are those planes, I am
one that has been shot down again and again. This
repeated itself for over 15 years because I was not that
good at sales and didn't enjoy how I was selling. So I left
the profession entirely to publish this book.

But through it all I somehow won Rookie of the Year and
Top Performer awards. I closed sales over $500,000 and
had territories with revenue of more than $5 million. I
averaged total compensation in the six figures in 13 of my

15 years in sales. I also worked for some of the biggest and best technology companies. However, a lot of this success came from luck and circumstance. If someone really wanted to know how to sell, I am the last person they should speak to.

I realized, all I am qualified to do, is teach people how *not* to sell.

When it comes to the subject of sales, hundreds of books have been written by countless salespeople who focus almost entirely on the times they've won and how they overcame different obstacles. Few want to talk about the times they failed. Not only are these books not in touch with reality and the fact that you will lose a lot in sales, they also give a false sense of how you can win. This is because the problem with following those who have succeeded is that it's difficult to apply what they've done to your situation, and there's usually a variable that led to their success that can't be taught.

I'm a failed salesman admitting all my mistakes to teach you how to do it right. By listening to me, rather than implement a list of seemingly correct actions to improve your sales skills, you can learn from me by removing incorrect actions. This is better because, one, it takes less work to not do something, and two, it gives you the space to see what you want to add that makes the most sense for you.

Here are some of the ways that this book is different than other sales books:

- In Chapter 2, you'll learn why a salesperson's skills are not half as important as how good their territory is.

- In Chapter 3, you'll learn the true nature of managers, and that the best you can hope for is that they don't make you miserable.
- In Chapter 4, I'll share how terrible I was at networking and preferred to use the most useless method of prospecting: email.
- In Chapter 5, I'll recap the types of decision makers you'll encounter, and how I did a poor job of working all of them.
- In Chapter 8, I'll talk about how I did the grave mistake of emailing proposals instead of getting in front of my customers.
- In Chapter 10, you'll learn how to navigate between different jobs because you will move around a lot in sales (you might even get a PIP).

Moreover, I'll talk about why I was unable to form the relationships one needs to close more deals, and the ethical dilemmas I faced along the way.

All this is geared towards the following people:

- Those contemplating a career in sales or are early in one
- Those not in sales but need help in it to support another profession
- Those good at sales but want to reinforce the basics (or want a good laugh)
- Those looking for an honest story

Positive asymmetry

The concept of asymmetry was introduced to me from the incredible book *Antifragile* by Nassim Taleb. The book talks about how a person can rarely predict an event that brings a negative effect to their life, but they can predict how fragile they are to that event to minimize its impact or even benefit from it. Think of a person who doesn't know if the stock market will crash but is invested in a way where a crash increases the amount of their portfolio.

One way to be "antifragile" is to make decisions that result in positive asymmetry, meaning it has more upside than downside. Trying something new usually has positive asymmetry. A friend may offer to take you to an art museum when you don't think you care much for art. But if you have no plans, why not go? The upside is that you have a good time and meet interesting people, realize you like art and now have a new hobby, and you walk out of the museum feeling creative and think of a great idea. On the downside, you lose a few hours if you don't leave sooner.

This book is rife with positive asymmetry. At worst, you'll lose some time and a few bucks. At best, you will be entertained and pick up several tips that will help your sales career. You might also realize sales isn't what you want to do and end up pursuing another profession. You can really only gain by reading this book.

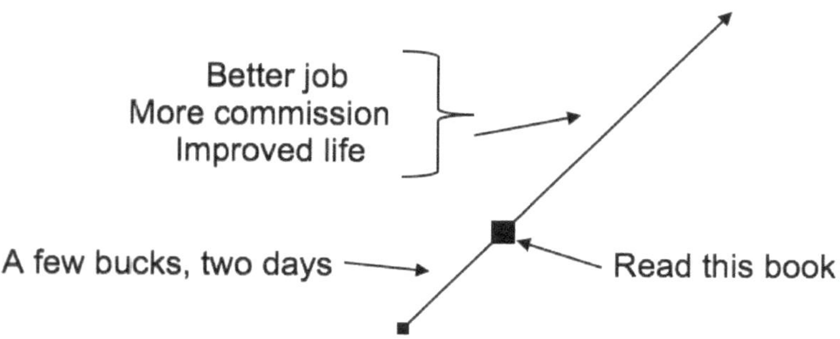

I wrote this book to share my experiences while I was a salesman. I want to tell my story and help others. I hope what you read makes you think hard about whether sales is the right career for you, helps you in that career, and along the way makes you laugh. Read this book because I've seen it all and I'm willing to share it in an honest way.

And if you don't like the book, then you actually think it's great. Remember, the title is: How *Not* to Sell.

Chapter 1: Get Experience

*The only source of knowledge
is experience.*

-Albert Einstein

When starting a sales career, or any career, it's essential to get your first job to gain experience. It might not be the best job but you need it to eventually get a better one. More importantly, that first sales job will help you determine whether you are good at sales and if you like it. You might not realize either thing right away but as you progress you'll naturally think and feel if it's a career path you want to continue. The challenge with sales, like most new endeavors, is that you will run into resistance early. You will be rejected and often feel lowly. You might also do things you don't feel are ethical, as I talk about in Chapter 12. But you could make sales, feel great from the praise you get from others, and be accepted as a part of a community. The important part is to stick with it for long enough to where you can honestly say whether it is right for you.

The start of it all

I had the makings of a salesman as far back as senior year of high school when I sold credit cards for MBNA Bank. I'll never forget going into their office at 17 and selling a product I wasn't old enough to have. The goal was to get one person an hour to sign up for the card I was selling that day. I had a 1.5 card per hour average, which was better than many others that had been doing the job for much longer than me. Not only was I successful, but I also had a lot of fun. My earliest memory of the hilarity of sales was the day I was selling the NFL credit card, which had a logo of whatever team a person wanted and got them extra benefits to use towards team merchandise and tickets. I was given a script that had a blurb to say about each team as I called into their respective city. When I got to the San Diego Chargers, I read "pretty uniforms," and burst out laughing thinking about calling some drunken guy in San Diego and saying, "How about those Chargers and their pretty uniforms!"

I also had my first taste of failure in sales at MBNA. I called a guy in Texas who said he was very interested in a card. As we went through the application his enthusiasm for it kept growing – to the point where he was celebrating. When we got to the annual income section he yelled out "$250,000!" I was so excited that I was going to get him to sign up. Little did I know he was pulling my leg and at the end of the call, right before he was to agree to the terms and conditions, he hung up the phone. I felt stupid but learned not to tie my personal worth to whether I made a sale (a lesson I wish I followed more later in my career).

The experience working at MBNA gave me my first cases of closing a sale, losing a sale, and everything in between. It was just a pretense of what was to come.

How to get there

The job with MBNA was an important step for me in becoming a salesman. In addition to letting me know that I liked sales and was good at it, it also helped build my resume to get my next job. My sales career started before it even began, even though I didn't know it at the time. It's important for you to do this too. Building up a resume and list of experiences will be what will lead to the next step. It doesn't even have to be a job. Whether you are still in college or looking for a job at 40, it's important to immerse yourself in different activities. Not only will you be doing what you love, but it will also open you up to new opportunities. You've got to put yourself into things you enjoy to lead to what you eventually want. But it also takes some luck.

As I'll explain in the next chapter, success in sales has a lot to do with luck and circumstance. I believe this because I've experienced it and seen it with others my entire life. My first taste of it was at the end of my junior year of college. I had no idea what I was going to do that summer. I had changed my major to Communication Systems Management (CSM) and was considering switching back to Political Science when just a week before summer break, WorldCom, then one of the largest telecommunication companies in the country, called me to do an internship in Dallas, TX. While I was there I was getting paid $18 an hour and the internship solidified my resume to get a job after I graduated.

How did I get that internship? The manager in charge of selecting the intern was an Arab Muslim. I'm sure from my name he mistakenly assumed I was too and picked me from a stack of resumes because of that. I was an average, first year CSM student who had no contact with WorldCom before learning I was chosen. There was not much that made me stand out or worth being chosen over others aside from Anwar's preference to help a fellow "Muslim." I can't say this is bad since people usually want to take care of those they identify with, but it shows how luck and circumstance had as much to do with me getting it as my resume.

Upon graduating, working at WorldCom was not an option since the company went bankrupt shortly after my internship and the telecommunication industry went down with it. With few options, I went to Chicago to interview for different sales jobs. I didn't know what I wanted to sell but I knew I wanted to live in Chicago. I was open to selling anything since I liked sales and could make good money doing it. And whatever I was selling, what I really wanted was more experience. Several opportunities didn't work out but I remained optimistic. Towards the end of my stay in the Windy City, I visited and accepted a sales job with Thermal-Chem, a small, privately owned business in the Chicago suburb of Franklin Park. Little did I know where that job would lead.

Get that first job

Thermal-Chem manufactures epoxy coatings used to repair and resurface concrete floors. It wasn't the most glamorous job. My salary was $2,000 a month plus minimal commissions and I spent two hours in traffic every day. I was selling to blue-collar businesses and contractors in the Chicagoland area. Two of those contractors, Louie and Ray, might have been part of the mafia or at least acted like it. It was a dirty job, literally, that often had my hands in glue-like substances and my nose inhaling chemicals. But I liked the job and continued to enjoy the dynamic nature of sales. I also gained a lot of experience that taught me how to sell and kept me in the profession. Many of the valuable lessons I learned I didn't always follow later in my career, including the following:

Learn to walk away

Later in the book I write more about how walking away from certain opportunities is something salespeople need the strength to do. It's equivalent to poker where the best players can fold a hand they could win because the reward is not worth the risk. An early example of this came from calling on Sauk Machine Works, a contract machining company in Wheeling, IL, which has since been purchased by another company. The owner Michael needed to coat the floors of his brand new 20,000 square foot warehouse to protect it against wear and tear but he didn't want to pay full price to do it. I brought in a contractor who felt $2 per square foot, or $40,000, was a fair price, which it was. But not to Michael. He wanted $.50 per foot and after much back and forth we settled on $.85. The job turned out to be a disaster. Because the contractor had to use less material to make a profit, the floor ended up uneven and discolored. Michael was furious and demanded we come back to finish the job properly. The contractor did and we ended up losing money on the project.

I wish I could go back to this deal more than any other in my career, just to walk away. I would tell Michael to his face how shortsighted he was being. He just invested in a warehouse that was going to be the center of his operations for decades yet he wasn't willing to put in a little extra cash to properly protect it. But instead of standing up to him by saying what he needed to hear and creating some tension (something important to do as I'll explain in Chapter 6) I curled my tail between my legs and gave him what he wanted. I was excited to get a sale and scared to confront him. But I knew what he was paying was not fair, and I learned that cutting corners is not good in sales even if it does make you a commission.

See the job through

I write more in Chapter 9 about working deals beyond the point when the sale is made. I first learned this at Thermal-Chem. I landed a deal with G&K Services, a laundromat with several locations across Chicago. We were tasked with coating the floors of one location to reduce the amount of dust. We inked the deal but I stopped doing anything after that. On the day the contractor was doing the work, I was sitting in my apartment hanging out with friends. I got a call from the customer who came to see the work and he was yelling about how the yellow lining that directed people where to go was misapplied. I was completely reactive to the situation and had to call the contractor and drive out to the location to see what they had done. The problem was not resolved quickly and the customer was so disappointed that I did not get the business at any of the other locations.

This is a basic lesson that when you make a sale the work is not done until you've seen the project all the way through. I should have known what the customer wanted and been on location to meet the contractor to ensure everything was done correctly. I should have been there to meet the customer after to walk through everything to ensure he was happy. If a mistake was still made at least I am there to smooth things over and to try and fix it quickly. This was my success on the line and I didn't do the required work beyond closing the sale.

Don't give a price

Chapter 7 covers not being so quick to give a price. It's better to find out the customer's budget and establish value for your product before you throw out a cost. This was a mistake I committed many times in my career that I should have learned once at Thermal-Chem and rarely done again. My manager had given me a sweet lead that should've been an easy close. In talking to the customer, he asked me what the cost would be for the project. Since I hadn't seen the work I didn't have enough information to give an accurate cost but he pressed me so I went ahead and told him what to expect. When my manager found out he was incredulous that I gave a price before seeing the job. Sure enough when we went to see the work it was going to cost more than the high end I estimated. But the customer worked to hold us at our price before we negotiated somewhere in the middle. We got the deal but had I waited to see the project I could have started at the higher, correct price and held there.

Take a risk

Thermal-Chem also taught me about taking risks, which salespeople will do, for example, in taking a new job, as I'll talk about in Chapter 10. A year into Thermal-Chem I was making decent commissions but not as much as I could have because it was Thermal-Chem who paid me and not the contractors. The contractors paying me was forbidden by Thermal-Chem since they were worried it would make me partial to specific ones and cause bidding wars. I knew I could make more money if the contractors paid me so I approached my boss and told him I wanted to forgo my base salary and negotiate a deal to collect commissions from both Thermal-Chem and the contractor. He agreed.

This was a risky move since I'd no longer have any guaranteed money. Looking back, I can't believe I gave up a base salary. But it did allow me to work from home and not need to spend time and money commuting to an office. The results were initially disastrous because I decided to do this in January, which was the slowest time of the year because of the cold weather. It was a good idea with poor execution. I spent the next three months with little income. Thankfully, the move finally paid off once it got warm.

Every salesperson needs their Thermal-Chem. They need that company where they are going to grind out sales and learn what the game is really like. No one in any profession starts at the top and sales is no different. This is just some of what I learned in my first job out of college. The experience I gained at Thermal-Chem was invaluable to starting my sales career. Not only for the lessons I learned and the situations I was exposed to, but to add to my resume to get my next job; one that launched my career to the next level.

The big time

Without the experience of Thermal-Chem I would not have gone on to get a job at Pearson Education. Pearson is the world's largest publisher of educational materials and jobs with them are not easy to get. It was a stroke of luck that I even got an interview. I had no idea textbook publishers existed let alone that they had jobs for 24 year olds to travel to college campuses and sell books to professors to use in their classes. A close friend got a job with Pearson in another city through Craigslist of all places and lucky for me I got a referral from him. I still had to do the work to get the job and I prepared as thoroughly as possible for the interview. At this point I had $200 in my bank account and I was desperate to get the job.

My bank account went to $50 after I purchased a $100 suit and $50 shoes from Aldo to wear for the interview. It went well but I was informed the next day that I would not be getting the job. I went to return the shoes that now had huge creases in the front. The store refused to take them back so I emailed the corporate office to complain, and, fortunately, they took the shoes back. That's how low things got for me but at least my bank account was back to $100.

As further luck would have it, Pearson called me a few days later and told me they liked me and now had two jobs they could offer. One was for a territory with the inside sales team, which would allow me to stay in Chicago. The other was for an outside territory that would require me to move to Northwest Ohio, two hours from where I grew up but a very rural area. It was a tough decision since I didn't want to leave Chicago but I chose the outside territory because it offered a car, higher salary, the ability to work outside of an office, and I figured, like working at Thermal-Chem, it would lead to something bigger. Also, although I didn't know it at the time, that option had way more upside than the inside job. It was one of the best career decisions I've ever made, as I'll explain in the next chapter.

Diversify yourself

Throughout this book, a lot of the examples come from the education industry, which is where I spent most of my career. It's common for salespeople to work almost entirely in one industry. This happens because once you start in one industry, it's natural to stay there. You'll end up learning things specific to that industry and if you move to another company it will likely be to a competitor. Once you get in several years with an industry it's going to be hard to get a job in another industry at the level you want since that new company likely prefers to hire someone with industry experience. But having experience mainly in one industry doesn't narrow my sales knowledge, because regardless of what you are selling or to whom, many of the strategies, dynamics, and processes are similar. What are different are the nuances, which you will learn with time.

In over 15 years of being in sales, I sold to three distinct industries. I've sold physical products, technology services, marketing solutions, platforms for app development, media, and more. I've sold to dozens of titles including professors, executives, marketing managers, owners, company presidents, and creative directors. This diverse experience makes up the stories in this book.

If you can diversify yourself it will help your sales career. It's beneficial since if your current industry goes stale, you'll have options. I'm sure the folks at WorldCom realized this after their bad luck of being part of an industry that collapsed. There are ways to diversify. You can take classes while you're working where you learn another skill set. I could get a sales job with Salesforce, one of the largest technology companies in the world, when I didn't have the experience because I had learned their product in previous jobs. You can also find a job that requires you to wear many hats. I know people that worked in marketing or product development and then transitioned to sales because the jobs required similar skill sets. Keeping a large network also helps since you might need to ask for a favor from someone to help get you an interview or provide a reference.

Do you like sales?

I advocate learning by doing. There's little that will teach you more about sales and life than experiences. But that might not be possible if you are just starting your sales career. This is where books like this and other outlets can help. You can pick things up from the successes and failures of others to apply to your life. Join a club or networking group that is sales centric. Read sales books, watch movies about sales, and talk to others in sales. These are great ways to learn about sales and prepare for interviews, as it will give you something to show your interviewer you are working to improve. While writing this book I looked at dozens of other sales books and thought about how much better I could have been had I read some of them when I was selling. Ones that stood out are *The Sales Bible*, *SPIN Selling*, and *To Sell is Human*. I'll reference some of the resources I found in this book.

Once you get experience, you need to decide if sales is for you. If you don't like it and don't have success after a reasonable amount of time, then the choice is easy. Few gamblers lost the first time they played because if they did, they wouldn't have kept playing. But if you are good then you'll probably want to stay. You will close deals and make a lot of money. You'll have a great lifestyle and have fun. You'll validate yourself by being able to beat others and win the deal. But you might also manipulate people. You might build relationships that center around your desire to sell something and where your worth is predicated on how much revenue you generate. You might be part of a corporate structure that demands you generate more profit and more growth to the detriment of yourself and society. Either way you must accept it all to truly love it. The time to decide if this is the life you want is now. What will it be?

Chapter 2: Get a Good Territory (and Some Luck)

Luck is what happens when preparation meets opportunity.

-Vince Lombardi, legendary coach
of the Green Bay Packers

When starting a sales job, developing your territory takes time. Belief in yourself and patience are critical in order to stay motivated as you follow your chosen strategies. According to a 2015 report on sales development and recruitment from CA Technologies, one of the world's leading software development companies, it can take as long as 12 months for a sales rep to become fully productive. Smart companies recognize this and provide their new hires a ramp-up period where they have a reduced quota. It's the best time in a rep's job since not much is expected of them, however, it's also the most important time since the foundational work needs to be done to build towards those sales by the end of the first year and beyond.

One book that gives a guide on how to start in your territory is *Sales Hunting: How to Develop New Territories and Major Accounts in Half the Time Using Trust as Your Weapon* by David Monty. Monty makes the case that since other vendors have already established relationships within the accounts you're selling to, a new sales rep will not make any sales until they establish their own trust. Monty then provides ways to do this by quantifying relationships on a spreadsheet and providing a structured map to follow. Monty is a 20+ year IT salesman who has proven success. He even resigned from the job he had at the time he published his book in order to take a job with another company where he could practice from scratch what he preached (something highly respectable). In his first year doing this he finished at 230% of his yearly quota.

Another great book by the aforementioned Nassim Taleb is *Fooled by Randomness: The Hidden Role of Chance in Life and in the Markets*. The book investigates the role that "luck, uncertainty, probability, human error and risk" play in our lives and the business world. One of the main ideas is that often, the people that make it to the top get there because of sheer luck and circumstances. We mistake successful people for being brilliant when it's not always their skills that got them to the situation they are in as much as it was the situations they were in that helped them reach greatness.

This is what Monty's book and others don't tell you about how salespeople can become successful. It does take hard work. It takes discipline and thoughtful strategy. It requires art and skill. But it also takes immense luck and circumstances that are in your favor. In Monty's case, he is advocating to do what he did and success is all but guaranteed. He even proved it by following his book exactly and blew out his sales goal in his first year. Although he doesn't say what he did in year 2 and beyond, or what the circumstances of his territory were that lead to his initial success. I'm not saying that the circumstances were the only cause, but there's no doubt that much of it can be attributed to the specifics of his territory. Certainly, a defined standard applied to all territories of how to succeed is not going to work for everyone. Each salesperson needs to determine what's best for them and their territory, and it takes a little luck along that path for it to work.

Luck and circumstances

During my career, I've made big sales and in some years, I've missed my quota by the same amounts. The experiences on both sides are the basis for the lessons in this book. Whether I've succeeded or failed I've mainly followed the same work ethic and employed the same tactics. What was different was the situation I was in. I had sales territories where success was inevitable and territories where failure was unavoidable. I've come to learn that success in sales is more about luck and circumstance than art and skill.

Whether I was set up to succeed or not, I was still required to perform basic functions and avoid certain actions that would or would not result in a sale. Art and skill do play a role. If I could get a sales territory that was ripe to do well I still needed basic sales acumen to close a deal. I also had to create my own luck by finding the right territory that brought about the better chance for success. On the other hand, if a territory was doomed, I still needed to be good enough to cover myself to remain in the position until a better job came up.

Keep in mind that much of life is luck and circumstance. We are all born into a world we did not choose that may or may not come with advantages. If you are born to wealthy parents or within a healthy environment that cultivates success, your chances of being successful increase significantly. One can work himself out of poverty or lose the silver spoon they were handed from the start, but these are exceptions that only prove the rule.

Throughout my career, the most important factor to my success (or failure) was the circumstances of my territory. I showed how luck got me the internship at WorldCom and then the job at Pearson. When I started at Pearson in August of 2004 I had no manager and little knowledge of how to effectively work my accounts. But I worked hard. I was making 15 in-person sales calls every day. I was sending another 20 emails a day across my territory of 10 accounts, which contained upwards of 500 customers. I worked every night and weekend. I put myself out there even as I wasn't sure my actions were leading to success. After all that it was the luck of my territory that brought my real success. As the calendar year ended and sales were coming in, one of my customers accidentally placed an order three times in our system for a book I had sold them.

Luck via human error randomly came into my territory with an order that was worth $51,000 that was meant to be only $17,000. I ended up finishing $50,000 over my goal instead of $16,000. No one questioned the sale because they didn't know there was something wrong with it or they didn't care. All that mattered was that I got the sale and surpassed my goal. The result of that was immense for me. Not only did I make an additional $3,500 in commission but I was viewed as an up and coming star of the company. I got a lot of attention. I was thought to be a great salesperson and in turn that perception became reality. People noticed me and gave me their time and resources that I likely would not have received if that order was for just $17,000 and I barely made my goal. Thanks to the support received from others, I went on to crush my sales quota in 2005 and won the Rookie of the Year award.

My success in 2005 was from more than just that support. I closed many other sales due to the circumstances of the territory. Since it was in a rural area, there were few competing reps that were on campus as much as I was. I inherited a strong base of customers and several of the books they were using were going into new editions that year, which got me a ton of orders. In 2006 I also made my sales goal in part to Pearson merging with one of its biggest competitors. The newly formed company started giving credit for sales to the reps of both of the previous companies if it was agreed that one would back off when the other was close to closing a sale. They figured if both reps were selling against each other a third competitor could sneak in and win it. That policy led to me getting credit for a $150,000 deal I didn't even win. After all that success I was promoted to a new territory in Chicago where the circumstances kept playing a huge role.

I started in the new territory in August of 2006 and was given a goal for the rest of the calendar year. But this time the opposite took place of what happened in 2004. I finished at 84% of my quota as I inherited a territory that had been underworked for several years. It was a rough few months as Pearson expected a lot more from me, but I was patient because I knew big things were coming. In fact, I didn't want any sales so I'd have a lower sales number and quota to compete with in the following full year.

I wanted the new territory not just to move back to Chicago but also because I knew that it was an underworked territory and had great potential to make a lot of sales and a ton of money. That's exactly what happened. I used the end of 2006 to get to know my customers. I showed my face a lot and asked questions without directly selling anything. They hadn't seen a salesperson from the company or any of our products in years. By the start of 2007, they were lining up to use my books in their classes. I hustled a lot and was all over my territory selling everything I could but my success didn't have as much to do with my skills as me being in the right territory at the right time. Since the territory was down in previous years it was going to bounce back to some degree, regardless of who was working it. I was able to take advantage of that to the highest degree. I finished $700,000 over my goal earning me a $50,000 bonus check and Top Performer honors. After that I was promoted again, this time to a district sales manager position. At 27, I wasn't qualified for that job but my track record said otherwise. I was also lucky to be in the right place at the right time since the position had been open for three years and they were anxious to hire someone. I sensed another opportunity to make a lot of money so I took it, and I'll talk more about what happened in the next chapter.

The flip side

Unfortunately for others, sales is a zero-sum game. While I reaped the benefits of these territories, the reps that followed me did not fare as well. They were unlucky to inherit very challenging situations that were going to be nearly impossible to succeed in. Let's start with the rep that followed me in Ohio. She had to increase sales in a territory where I had won Rookie of the Year and it was going to be difficult to find more sales to do that. She also had to contend with the sale made by the competing company that I got credit for that was still in her base number even though they were no longer going to do joint credit. She had no idea when she got the job how bad of a situation she was getting. She might have been the best salesperson in the company but her territory's circumstance made it difficult to prove this.

The Chicago territory was inherited by a young and ambitious woman who had been working for several years in the company as an inside rep. There was no reason she shouldn't have been successful except for the fact that she couldn't have received a worse territory. Her goal was going to be impossible to hit since I had increased sales by $700,000 the previous year and there was no more room for growth. The difference in these two cases is that the Chicago rep knew what she was getting into. She was just so eager to move to an outside territory that she didn't care. But had she really thought about what she was in for I don't think she would have taken the job. Four months after I moved into the manager role, I received a call from the VP of Marketing telling me that her customers were saying I lied to them about what I promised related to the books I had sold them. What they were saying wasn't true and they were just trying to take advantage of her to get things for themselves, and she had to protect herself by making up more lies about what I had done. She left the job and company a few months after that.

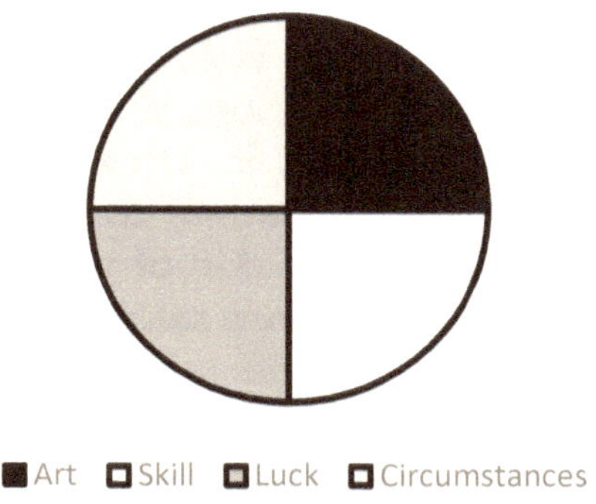

Happens to others

I've seen circumstance affect people not in sales, too. When I worked in advertising for EyeWonder, I closed a deal where we were tasked to run the online media ads for Kentucky Fried Chicken's new grilled chicken option. The creative agency would create the ads and send them to us to place on the Internet. The project turned out to be a mess as the creative agency proved less-than-expert at creating online ads and they had to rescind a printable coupon for two free pieces of chicken. Our company ended up redoing everything. At one point the creative agency threw me under the bus and said I was responsible for a delay in creating some of the ads. After all that drama, the campaign was considered a major success, as Adweek reported that KFC increased overall sales by 10% in the quarter during which the grilled chicken was launched. Some at the company said this was because of the coupon fiasco, not in spite of it, because it gave the company so much free publicity. It also helped that KFC already had a huge base of customers, making it inevitable that the grilled option would be a success. Lucky for the creative agency's team, they had an easy "territory" that could do all the work for them. But six years later they lost the KFC account. This shows that while luck can get you sales and bring other success, it's not the only ingredient.

Even as I write this book I am witnessing the luck of sales with a colleague. A rep on his team in Oregon took a job with another company. This was a surprise and it left the regional manager having to go through the lengthy process of finding a replacement. While the territory was open, the colleague was asked to cover it and in return he would receive commission for any sales that were closed. It just happened that the previous rep was working a deal worth $400,000 that was far along in the process. The colleague finished the deal and in addition to getting full credit for it, he made a $40,000 commission check for a few weeks of work. It may have taken real effort and skill to complete the deal but he inherited a well-qualified opportunity that not only made him a ton of money but also goes towards his final yearly number that all the executives would see.

At the end of the year, do you think those executives looked at his number and said, or even knew, that one of his biggest deals was given on a silver platter? Will they realize how lucky he was and how it was the circumstance that led to his success? No, all they cared about is what all executives care about, which are the final results, and then showered him with praise. That's what happened as he finished 150% of goal and was the poster boy for what it takes to win the big deal. There's no question his skill was responsible for closing other deals but that doesn't change the fact of how lucky he was.

I'll include one last example. As I write this, another sales rep I know just closed two sales for $90,000 in his third month on the job. Both opportunities were add-ons, meaning a customer he inherited decided to purchase more products on top of what they were already using.

When he told me more about the sale, I learned that the customer first reached out to someone in the company who was completely unrelated to the territory. That message was forwarded to someone else who doesn't cover the account until finally reaching the correct rep. He completed the order and will receive a $4,500 commission check for something a 20-year-old intern could have processed.

This example also shows how the sales rep was three months into the job and hadn't even reached out to that customer to introduce himself and let them know he is their contact. On top of these sales he had a few others he admitted fell into his lap to total a $123,000 month. He finished at 200% of his quota and won Rookie of the Year. This is the benefit of having a prime territory. I know the feeling because at one company I was given credit for a $30,000 sale I had nothing to do with in my third month. I didn't even know that the product existed until it was sold!

These are just some of the cases I've seen that show that the territory you get is of the utmost importance to the success of a sales rep. You can be the best salesperson in the world, or mediocre, and that is not half as important as the situation you are in. This is what sales brought others and me, and can bring you. By entering the "game," salespeople are subject to earning massive amounts of money by being in the right place at the right time. Some might say that this is too narrow of a view and it doesn't consider everything done prior to getting to that position and the sales that fell into our laps are a result of previous hard work. In all the examples, each person created their own luck to put themselves in the position they were in to benefit. And not all sales will be this easy and skill will win out in the end. That is true, but it's even more true that without a good territory the opportunity to get those deals will be harder to come by.

Here's the formula for success I've outlined so far:

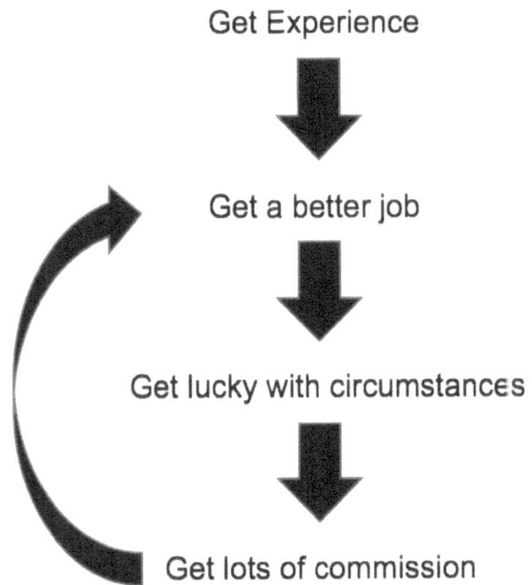

Not always good luck

This has worked on the other side for me on many occasions. There were times when no matter what I did, my territory is why I failed. I experienced this in 2014 when I went to work for Wiley Education. I took the job because they were paying me $25,000 more a year and it was a promotion to a better title. But the company had a public relations nightmare a few months before I took the job when their technology had failed on their customers, causing a lot of chaos. This information was publicly available prior to me taking the job but I never bothered to do the research to possibly realize this. In this case, I failed to properly prepare. If I had I might have decided against accepting the job since my position was as a Digital Learning Specialist and I was going to deal with many unhappy, distrustful customers. Much like the positive luck I previously stepped into, this was negative luck.

For the next year and a half I was supporting a team of 12 sales reps and I had just a few large sales. For seven years before that I was successfully selling within higher education and now I could hardly make a sale to save my life. I was starting to think that all my luck was catching up to me and showed my true colors but I don't believe that is entirely accurate since there's no doubt I should have made more sales in that role with my background. Poor preparation got me into the job but the circumstances of the company were what led to my failings. The fact that our technology was not trusted played a huge role. On top of that, the sales reps I was supporting were average performers. Only 3 of 12 made their sales goal in that year. No one who had my role in that territory would have done any better.

For me, I can't stand not making sales so I moved from that role to a sales job with Colloquy, where I was selling educational technology services to C-level executives. It was a big step up from my previous job in terms of who I was calling on and it was a job I was not qualified for at the time. I just happened to know a person in the company who got me the interview. I hit it off with the hiring manager and after an interview with an indifferent company president, I got the job and was now making an even higher annual salary.

Once again, I didn't know what I was getting myself into. I soon learned that many at Colloquy were as apathetic as the president. There was no chance anyone would have been successful there and I know this because I saw or heard of 8 sales reps come and go from the company in the year I was there. Colloquy had a revenue loss of $25 million since it started 5 years before I was hired. I learned most people were there just to collect a bloated salary and had no interest in taking on a new customer and doing any real work. I didn't know it when I was hired but I walked into a situation where there was no chance for success. It didn't matter if I was the greatest salesman on the planet; I was not making a sale. I left 13 months after I started. Not long after that Colloquy was sold.

Here's another formula for success:

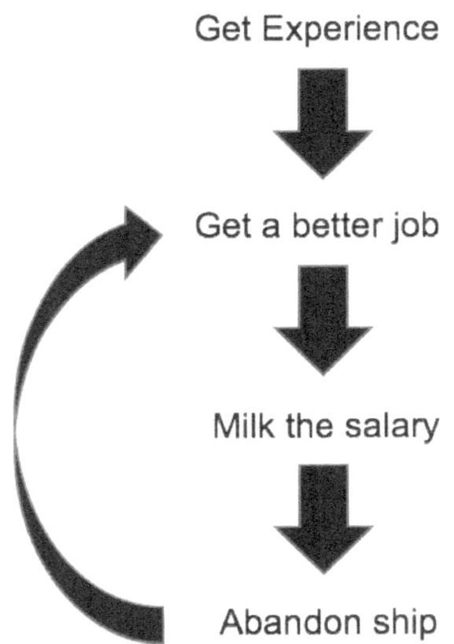

Arbitrary salesman

There's a story from Greek mythology about the Procrustean bed. Procrustes, the son of Poseidon, was an evil guy who had an outpost on an important path that stretched between the cities of Athens and Eleusis. When travelers were on this path, Procrustes would invite them to spend the night in his guest bed. They would soon realize the trap when Procrustes would force his guests to fit the size of the bed by either stretching them if they were too short or cutting off their legs if they were too tall. The adage represents the idea of a person trying to fit something into an arbitrary standard. For example, you might not need to drink 8 glasses of water everyday.

This was the mistake I made later in my career. I didn't fit the beds of the jobs I lied in, but I still forced myself into them. Although I worked in higher education for 12 years, I started taking jobs in the industry that I wasn't prepared for, which led to my failures. My failures led to my unhappiness with the positions I was in, which led to my eventual exit from the profession altogether.

In these jobs I was selling products I was not familiar with to customers I could not relate to. I took these jobs arbitrarily and not based on the standard I had set up for myself in the previous seven years. When I went to work for Colloquy I was calling on vice presidents for marketing, enrollment, student success, and alumni relations when I had never sold a solution to those areas or worked in them. My experience had been selling textbooks and classroom technology to professors. But I took the higher-level job because I found a way to get it and because it paid a good salary. I only took the job because it was sales job.

This continued with Blackboard but more notably at Salesforce. The position with them required five years of experience selling CRM software. I barely had two, but again, I took the job not because it was the right fit, but because it was a such a well-known company and because I was shrewd enough to get it. But even if it was something I considered to be my dream job, it was not something I was qualified for at the time, and in turn, it left me feeling inadequate and unhappy for not being able to do it well. It's best to know what your skill set is appropriate for rather than try to fit it into something it's not.

A better path to success would have been to work in higher education and then move to selling to those people. Many of the best salespeople spend time on the client side where they work in the positions of the people they are now selling to. This helps them understand their business, speak their language, and empathize. I could have also opened up to people already in those jobs when I was just a textbook salesman. I could have been educated by them to see what it takes to be successful in the jobs I eventually wanted. Instead, I just level jumped based on arbitrary standards that were not sustainable.

This bottom-up approach is the way to go in sales. It's best to gain experience incrementally and use it to grow naturally. The more you can sell something you know about the more you will not end up in the wrong position for the wrong reasons. This is like most of life. This book was written from the bottom-up. I do have the experience to create a sales book. 15 years of working the daily grind and being exposed to so many situations gives me the qualifications. Creating this just poured out of me in an organic way. It never felt difficult because I loved to do it and felt I was good at it.

Forcing things is like going to a dating site to find a relationship. This is coming from a top-down approach to find someone by looking at pages of singles with carefully crafted messages and criteria hoping to find one you like. To find real love, one can do it by focusing on what they like to do and meet people at those same places. It might just take longer until that special someone comes along. Similarly, it's like trying to change how your body looks. You can't do it in two weeks by lifting the heaviest weights and taking a pill. It requires daily work for months and years to improve it for the long term.

Find the right situation

Luck was something I created or didn't. To get the opportunity to make those sales, however they happen, you have to prepare yourself to get a great environment to succeed in. That's what I tried to do. I prepared as a competent salesperson and I found the right territory where there was opportunity. Or I didn't prepare and found a bad situation.

That's why it's as important as anything else during the interview process to ask intelligent questions about the territory and company. Not only for your own sake to know what you are getting into but also because it shows the hiring manager you are intelligent enough to ask a question beyond, "did the territory and company make its number last year?"

When you do find a job that fits your skill set, you need to interview smartly to determine what kind of territory and company you are getting. To know if it will go one way or the other, you need to know what questions to ask. Here are some of the key ones to ask and why to learn about the potential of a sales territory:

- Why did the last sales person leave? Where did they go? *If they are with the company it's less likely they fled the scene of a crime.*
- How has the territory performed over the last three years? *Hopefully the answer is that it's down. Ask why. Ask for specific numbers.*
- What kind of existing customers does the territory have? *Good if it has some sales to work with, but still plenty of upside.*
- What products have the company released in the last year or will release soon? *Find out if you'll have something new to sell and what need it's filling.*
- How has the company performed over the last five years? *Get to know if the organization is growing and will succeed overall.*

With the last two you might be able to learn that prior to the interview and modify your question accordingly. It's important to know if the company itself is positioned to do well. Had I researched Wiley and Colloquy more thoroughly I may have decided not to take those jobs. Even if Wiley gave me all the answers I wanted to hear about the territory, if the company is poor, then success is less likely. The territory might be down because of company mismanagement, which makes it harder to work back up. They may have new products coming out but if they are terrible, then it doesn't matter.

Luck is not limited to sales. The list of inventions discovered by accident is endless. The microwave came about when a Raytheon engineer noticed a chocolate bar in his pocket had melted when he stood in front of some radar equipment. A scientist who accidentally let mold contaminate one of his bacteria cultures when he left for a vacation led to him discovering penicillin. Velcro came about when a Swiss engineer was hiking and saw that burs were clinging to his pants and to his dog's fur.

So while luck can happen in any domain in life, the key is to keep putting yourself out there to let it find you.

Chapter 3: Get a Decent Manager

*When a flower doesn't bloom,
you fix the environment in which it grows,
not the flower.*

-Alexander den Heijer, inspirational speaker

Gardening is wonderful. You put a seed in the ground and provide good soil, water, and plenty of sun to watch it mature into a healthy plant. This is like all of life. Growth takes planting a seed in your mind and putting in the work until that growth manifests. Nothing happens overnight. Writing this book started with a thought and then took more than a year of daily work to complete. Like the plant, finishing the book required a supportive environment of a good editor and people who encouraged me. The same need for a supportive environment rings true for salespeople. You can be a promising salesperson, but put with unsupportive people you can easily fail. Likewise, a salesperson with little experience can grow to become successful if there are helpful people around her.

If the salesperson is the plant, the manager is the environment. The manager can nourish the rep and watch her grow, or do the opposite. If the manager is unhealthy soil that doesn't provide good training, the salesperson will not put down firm roots and sprout. If the manager withholds water and nourishment, the rep will never grow. If the manager is a harsh sun that beats down daily on the rep, they will become exhausted and die. In the domain of sales, the word environment can be replaced by culture. The culture that the manager creates is what will help or hurt the rep. If the culture is healthy, a rep will love their work and thrive. If the culture is toxic, a rep will become miserable and hate their life, and in turn sales can suffer.

I've seen this as a rep but it was most clear to me as a district sales manager at Pearson. The team had not made its collective number for three straight years. They also did not have a direct manager during that time. The team was run by a regional manager who was spread too thin to successfully lead a team of salespeople. It was apparent to me in the first week on the job that it wasn't the reps that were failing as much as the personnel and systems that were failing them. It took me a year to hire and fire the right people and implement training and other processes that fostered success. I left after that year but was informed to much regret that the team crushed its number the following year and I missed out on a large bonus check.

There's no shortage of books on sales management. As many books as there are teaching sales reps how to sell better, there are books teaching managers how to manage them better. One example is *ProActive Sales Management: How to Lead, Motivate, and Stay Ahead of the Game* by William "Skip" Miller. This is a practical book that covers all the basics for effective sales management including creating a positive culture, effective time management, motivation, coaching, and a favorite for the sales rep, reducing reports to one sheet of paper and 10 minutes a week. Sales management books are geared towards helping managers enhance the success of their reps. Although these books don't talk about how the manager is also destined to fail or succeed based on their circumstances. I'll leave that discussion to the books others write about management.

I have yet to find a book that is written from the salesperson's point of view on how they can help their manager. This book might be called "How to Make Your

Manager Successful." If this was written, it could be done in four words: make your sales goal. If you don't it will cost you your job. If you do, aside from the great money you'll make, you'll also be able to get away with virtually any type of poor behavior that would not be tolerated for another employee or sales person whose sales are lacking. I doubt I would have gotten away so easily when I mistakenly destroyed my company computer during my first year at Pearson if my sales numbers were not through the roof.

Types of managers

Before getting into specifics about how to recognize what kind of manager you will get and how to work with them, we need to define the most common types of managers. In the 15 years I've been selling I've had 14 direct managers and seen dozens of others. The reason I had so many wasn't as much to do with my moving between jobs as the fact that sales managers do the same (at Blackboard I had three managers in my first nine months). Companies will also restructure their sales forces resulting in reps moving to other teams. I have a pretty good sample size in my experience to break down most managers into the following five types:

The Buffoon

This person has no idea what they are doing and no one knows how they got to their position. They further prove the point that luck and circumstances play a huge role in getting people to where they are. They tow the company line very well and do exactly as they are told, which is always a prerequisite to climbing the management chain. They are nice and well-meaning but know little about sales. They can offer even less to help you close a deal. They love reports and are always asking you for things to be done by a certain date. They are reactive to every situation. They are scared, fragile people that will do anything to stay in their position. They are often over 40 and have a career filled with years of middle management roles.

The Prover

This person has the opposite personality and resume of the Buffoon. They are typically under 40 and they might be in their first management job following years of being a highly successful salesperson. They are hungry to prove they can manage. They try to instill fear in their reps while acting like they are part of the team and can empathize with you since they were also in sales. They have a lot of fake enthusiasm. They micromanage and insist you do things their way. They view any level of insubordination as disrespect. They love to fire reps they inherit as much as they love to hire new ones that they can train and mold to do exactly what they want. The latter case is why their manager hired them.

The Family Guy

The Family Guy is a good guy. He is as close to being the father figure that I will mention doesn't really exist with managers. He actually is a father and his kids are usually under 10. He's approachable, warm, and overall loved by his reps. It's just hard to get his attention because his personal responsibilities have him lose focus on the job. He is a bit aloof and stupid, but in a cute way. He takes little part in your deals so you are constantly telling him the same situation several times before it sticks. This leads to his manager being more involved with your deals than you'd like adding more pressure to your job. The Family Guy might be the most enjoyed manager by the rep that makes his number consistently and doesn't want to be bothered too much.

The Jerk

Not to be confused with the Prover, the Jerk enjoys making your life miserable. They either have no kids or all of them are in their teens or older. They put all the responsibility on their reps to make their number and then harass and blame them when they don't. Like the Buffoon, the Jerk can do little to help you close a sale and just expects it to get done. They will turn on you the first chance they get. Report only good news to this person, who will still turn it into something negative. The Jerk will pick a few reps on their team and support them while letting the others drown in misery. Their biggest enjoyment in the job is putting people on a Performance Improvement Plan (see Chapter 10 for more on PIPs).

The Nice One

This manager is as close to a mentor as you can get. I've only had this manager once and I must say I like this style. They have a lot of strong experience and have probably been with the company for many years. They like having a team that works closely together. They are patient and encouraging. They are a bit older and have a lot of close relationships with others, so like the Family Guy, you have to tell them something several times before they remember. They love to dominate sales calls and ramble on. But they do know their stuff. The main problem with the Nice One is they are so nice you are convinced it's an illusion and at any point they can call you out if you are not doing what they perceive as being correct.

Of the five types, the Nice One was clearly my favorite. The worst is not surprisingly, the Jerk. In my one year of management, I was the Prover. It's important to know yourself and what type will work best for you. A younger salesperson might need an aggressive Prover or even the Jerk to push (or scare) them to reach their full potential whereas a seasoned rep is best paired with the more hands-off Family Guy or Nice One. The Buffoon is worthless besides providing some good laughs at their expense. Whatever type you get, the manager will be very important in that they will or will not cultivate an environment that can help you. All of them require various ways to keep them and you happy. The one consistent thing is to keep making as many sales as possible. Other tips include not showing any sign that you are uninterested in your job or what the company is doing. Turn in reports on time. Have all the correct answers. Do everything you are told. Smile a lot and make them look good.

Interview your manager

Just like the territory, the type of manager a sales rep gets is based in large part on circumstance, even if you think you know them as you are interviewing. In every interview with a hiring manager I've asked what their management style is like, and I can say this is a worthless question. It sounds good because it seems like it would help you find out what you are getting into and if you two would get along. But all it does is create an illusion of predictability that you know what to expect. No manager will give you a truthful answer, and even if it is the truth, it might not last as circumstances change. He might tell you he is hands off and lets his salespeople have trust and autonomy, but when you are dealing with a high revenue deal, or your sales drop off for a month, he is micromanaging your every move.

Regardless of how the manager interviews you, it's the salesperson's responsibility to interview them rigorously. I recapped the key questions to ask about the territory in the last chapter. If they don't have clear answers for those questions, that is a red flag. The same goes for these questions to ask your potential manager:

- How would your reps describe what it's like working with you?
- Did you hire your current reps? Why?
- Why would you take this job if you were me?
- What should I know about you as a manager?
- What are your greatest and weakest attributes?

These are important questions you shouldn't be afraid to ask. If the manager is put off by you asking this, then just move on. Also, put as much attention on whether you like them as you do their answers. Was the conversation smooth? Did they treat you with respect? How did they respond if you didn't give the best answer? Were they open and honest in their replies? It's not much different than conversing with anyone and finding out quickly if there's positive energy and you sync well together. It's more qualitative than quantitative. Just let the conversation run naturally and ask yourself if you can see that person in your life on a near daily basis for the next few years. You should have multiple conversations with them during the process, which will help answer that.

Another effective way to find out what your manager is really like is to talk with another sales rep that reports to them so you can ask that person more pointed questions. Questions like, how often do you work with the manager? What's it like? Does he micromanage? If the manager is someone to avoid, another sales rep will let you know without explicitly saying to not take the job. Find out how long they and other reps have worked for him, and if the manager hired them. If they have been there several years, then chances are they really like the manager or else they would have left already.

It's a good sign if the hiring manager is the one suggesting interviews with other people. The jobs that work out best are ones where you talk to several people. This includes interviews with human resources, other managers, another salesperson, and a product specialist. This not only lets you ask a lot of questions to people in many different roles, but it also lets you understand what kind of company and people you are dealing with. It's also good to look for consistency in their answers.

To know what you are getting yourself into you must take the interview with your manager more seriously than they are taking it with you. To do this, try to flip the script by interviewing them. View them as the candidate for their job as your employer. If you can, try this:

Instead of:	They should:
You impressing them	Impress you
Them liking you	Be liked by you
You answering the next question	Get the next question from you
You following up	Follow up with you

The last one is a bit risky since they may not call, but shows you don't need them, which is a desirable trait. Just don't be so focused on getting the job that you overlook what kind of person you are going to work for. Don't be afraid to walk away if you smell something funny. There will be other jobs, and it's not worth putting your career at risk by investing a lot of time with someone, or something, only to find out later what you could have known before, which is that it's not the right fit.

I learned this the hard way when I left the education industry to go work in advertising at EyeWonder. I had already decided to leave my management job at Pearson to get the new job, and that became my sole focus. I completely overlooked whether the industry, job, and manager were right for me. I was mainly drawn by the allure of calling on media and creative agencies throughout downtown Chicago. The only rational reason I had for taking the job was because I thought it would be good to get out of higher education and get experience in a new industry, but I overlooked the fact that I had no experience working in advertising and that I completely dislike the field.

The position was the worst of the ten I had in my career. I went from being a district sales manager at one of the largest education companies in the world to putting together chairs during my first week at EyeWonder to set up the new office they had started renting. A month in, I was wrapping Christmas presents to take to a media agency. Nothing says "trust me" like getting a digital picture frame from someone you are meeting for the first time. The company provided little training and less structure for how deals would be worked. But worst of all, my manager had the work ethic of the Prover with the personality of the Jerk. We didn't get along, and it was difficult to work with under those conditions. I decided to cut my losses and leave after 11 months. It was obvious to me why many others from the sales team left during her time, and eventually her, too.

In hindsight, the reason this happened to me was clear. I never took the time to interview her the same way she didn't properly interview me. If we had we would have realized it was not the right fit. The interview was a meeting at a Google party when we were drunk. Most sales people might be happy when they get off with an easy interview, but this is a major red flag. A sales rep should want a disciplined interview. They shouldn't want a mean person but someone who is tough and fair in how they hire new talent. If this is the case, you can get a good sense from the interview as to what your manager will be like. At least you are starting from a place where you know the manager is no-nonsense but can end up being a great person, rather than a person who starts off easy going, and turns into something else.

A similar situation happened at Colloquy because I didn't pay attention to how easy it was to get the job. After being referred by a friend, I had a couple of conversations with the hiring manager. After that, I was invited to their home office where I had 30-minute interviews with the head of marketing, finance, and some random technical guy who couldn't have cared less if I got the job. I had one last meeting with the President who was late and gave me a softball interview. Two days later, I was offered the job. I didn't ask any questions. I just took it. But had I really thought about how easy it was to get the job, it might have sounded an alarm that I was getting involved with a shoddy company that was not going to be a long-term play. That's what happened as I explained last chapter. The lesson is if the job is easy to get, then it's probably not worth it.

Project or presentation

A sign of a strong company is one that has you do a project or final presentation that puts you in the role you are trying to fill. Before I was hired at Pearson and McGraw-Hill, both companies had me do a campus project where I was asked to go to a university in my area and call on professors as I would in the job. I then reported back what I learned. This was a great way to see if I enjoyed the job and let the company evaluate me on how intelligent and creative I was. At Salesforce, they had me deliver a presentation based on a case study like what I would encounter in the job. I had to present a PowerPoint to my manager and two others like I would in sales calls.

These companies are the ones I enjoyed working at the most and where I had the most success. Much of that was not just because those projects let me know what I was in for, but because they were reflections of a well-run company that knew how to screen for the right people.

These companies usually have the best managers because they were screened in the same way.

Trial week

Maybe the best idea I've seen to let an employee and employer know if it's the right fit comes from Sequoia, a company that supports other companies with seed money and staffing. Their hiring "secret" is Trial Week, which is exactly what it sounds like, where they have new hires work for a week at one of their partner companies. Trial Week allows Sequoia "to take chances on candidates who might not interview well and weed out people who make a good first impression but can't back it up." I would also think it gives the employee a unique way to determine if the company is right for them. Had I had a trial week with EyeWonder, I certainly would have run back to Pearson and groveled for my job back.

A trial week is something a sales rep can do even on their own when taking a new job. Before quitting your current job, start the new one and see what it's like. As in the case of Sequoia, take a week vacation or start the job at a time when it's less likely you'll be needed in your current job. The only risk is that it's possible your current company will find out, especially if it's a competitor where people across companies know each other and talk.

Working with your manager

As important as the manager is, do not rely on them for your success. It will be all up to you to close deals. Think of it as a sport where the coach can motivate and call plays, but it's on you as the player to perform. Prepare to be successful on your own or with support from others in your network. But working actual sales calls with your manager is going to happen. It can be a stressful situation. I did not look forward to the days when my manager was with me. I always felt everything had to be perfect. I needed appointments all day and each one had to be with the right people. I had to be perfectly prepared and know everything about our solutions, or look like I wasn't cutting it. But it doesn't always work like this. Sometimes a prospect cancels on you last minute. But if it happens on the day your manager is with you then it looks like you didn't set it up correctly. Sometimes I might not know the specifics about a product and my manager would wonder why. If you get a manager like the Prover or the Jerk, they will always be judging you no matter what they might say, so it adds a level of expectation that is not realistic.

What you can do to minimize this is at least a week prior to meetings, proactively set up a meeting with your manager. Review your agenda and goals, and ask what they think. Provide her with profiles of everyone you are meeting with. Give this information in detailed, concise chunks usually consisting of bullet points. Always have a PPT even if you don't think it's necessary in case she does and wants to help edit it. Always be more prepared for this meeting with your manager than for the actual meetings. But doing the former will help you prepare for the latter. In the actual meeting, let them talk and get them involved. You might as well use any expertise they can offer. Also, if the call goes bad, they can take some of the blame.

Not a friend

Another sales management book with an interesting approach is, *From Bud to Boss: Secrets to a Successful Transition to Remarkable Leadership* by Kevin Eikenberry. This book explains how sales managers who are now in a position of power can effectively supervise those that they were just on the same level as. I like this book because it's rooted in the reality that the manager and the people under him are not friends. He recognizes the inherent power structure and that there is a job to do above all else. Having strong relationships rooted in respect and trust are important, but this is not to be confused with friendship.

If you're lucky, your manager at best will be a coach or mentor and want to train, guide, and lead you since it will help you become a better salesperson, and overall better person. But no matter what your manager is like, they are not your friend, and certainly not a "father" figure. If you do have a personal relationship with your manager, understand that it will most likely be conditional on how strong your sales numbers are. The manager is your "friend" when your numbers are good but will not be quite so nice when they are not. They will not care about your personal life, and if they do, it will only be to reinforce their need to see you sell more. What they really care about is whether you are producing numbers that will help him make his goal so he can make money and satisfy his boss and the company. I'm not judging that this is wrong, I'm just saying that's the way it is.

An example is when I was with customers that I was close enough to that they asked me about my personal life. We were at lunch when my manager stepped away to take a call. One of the customers asked me how my relationship was with my girlfriend since they knew things with her were rocky. I told them we had recently broke up, and they were sympathetic. My manager came back and asked what we were talking about and one of the customers said my love life. They kiddingly asked him if he wanted the details and he said no. He jokingly said there might be an H.R. issue if we discussed too much and changed the topic to something related to work. But I don't think he was totally joking.

He might have been using the H.R. joke because he wanted to talk about work, he really was worried it might cause a personnel problem, or he just didn't care. I think it was the last option. He cared about the one thing most managers care about when it comes to their sales people, which is if they are making sales. His goal was to steer the conversation back to something work-related. He might have some genuine human emotion and felt sorry (especially if I had recent sales that make up for it) but it's short term and only done so that I'll get back to selling.

If your relationship with your manager feels like this, you can't sulk about it. You can't be offended or have your feelings hurt. You can't expect him to care, nor do you deserve any sympathy. This is the reality of being in sales.

You can't complain about it because it's the system you are choosing to be a part of. Understand that it's not really possible for him to care or for you two to have a meaningful relationship. The relationship is bound by the constraints of a sales goal and human resources manager, and you have to accept it, or get out.

In looking back on all of my managers, I am grateful for each one. I wouldn't have changed a thing about any of them. No matter if I liked them or didn't, or if they helped me or not, they all taught me a lot about myself. They all showed me what I want for my life and career, and without them, I would not be where I am today. I know that they had challenges too, and I wasn't always the best rep, but I hope they learned from me as well.

Chapter 4: Prospecting

Play the numbers. This is a contact sport. Meaning, the more people you contact the better you'll do.

-Nicky, from the movie *Boiler Room*

Now that you've got your job and your manager, you need leads. I have not found a subject that has more sales books dedicated to it than how to cold call and prospect for new business. Just search "prospecting" on Amazon, and you'll get dozens of pages of books, each with its own approach. Perhaps it's *Fanatical Prospecting: The Ultimate Guide to Opening Sales Conversations and Filling the Pipeline by Leveraging Social Selling, Telephone, Email, Text, and Cold Calling* by Jeb Blount. Just saying the title is hard work! Or perhaps your ticket is *Predictable Prospecting: How to Radically Increase Your B2B Sales Pipeline* by Marylou Tyler. Or even still, it could be *New Sales. Simplified: The Essential Handbook for Prospecting and New Business Development* by Mike Weinberg.

These many options support the idea of the survivorship bias that it's impossible to listen to any one person and feel confident that their method will be best. Maybe you need to follow Blount's 30-Day Rule, Law of Replacement, and Law of Familiarity. It could be Tyler's emphasis on a SWOT Analysis and the 4 P's. Or success could be behind the door of Weinberg's advice to prospect by telling stories. It's mind numbing to think of the many ways to go about this. We could listen to any of these "survivors" and think their success will be ours.

Luckily, most of these books are pretty much saying the same thing. There isn't much deviation from the central idea that prospecting takes part research, strategy, and hard work. In this chapter, I've simplified everything into one overarching structure for how to go about this essential task. From there, you can see what works for you. There's no need to spend countless days reading these books and trying to implement a dozen strategies. You can end up spending all your time doing one thing while all along another one would work better for you. Just follow a basic structure and as you go, find out what works for you and your territory, and proceed accordingly.

How to prospect

There are many ways to go about prospecting and generating leads, which needs to be a daily part of any salesperson's activities. There's no offseason to this. Even if sales are strong now, it's vital to keep producing leads that will become the sales of the future. Emailing, cold calling, and networking are the most popular ways to prospect. Leads can also come through word of mouth and referrals, which are in my opinion the most effective, and take the least amount of effort, as I'll explain.

In most companies I've worked at, email was the primary way I reached out to prospects to generate a pipeline of potential sales. I've sent several thousand emails over the course of my career using every tactic in the book to get a reply from a customer for a meeting. Based on all my experience I can say that sending emails is the least effective way to start the sales process. Before we get to that, let's talk about a couple of other things first.

When to prospect

Looking at it granularly, there's varying opinions about what days and times to prospect. Some say do it early in the day. You show you're a go-getter and people like that. If an executive gets a call from you at 7:30am, it shows that, like her, you are up early and work hard. They also might have more time for you the earlier you get to them. I'd much rather get my oil changed early in the day, or get the first flight out, so it's less likely delays come up as the day goes on. Calling early is also a good way to bypass the secretary since before they show up, that executive is more likely to answer their calls personally.

Calling early can set the tone for a great day by getting a new lead. It will keep you motivated. On the other side, you should prospect late. If you are making calls at 5:30pm, it also shows you work hard and can also bypass the secretary. It's equally a great way to end the day.

I've felt from my own experience that making calls on Monday is bad. People are busy, hate Mondays, and don't have the time or energy to take a call from a salesperson. It's best to make calls starting on Tuesday when potential customers are in the full swing of the week. Making calls on Friday is the best since you are likely to catch someone in a good mood with the weekend coming up. Make the calls between the :15 and :45 minutes of the hour so you catch them not in a meeting and not about to go to one.

There might be some truth to this, but you can throw most of it out the window. The thought that there is an ideal time of the day or week to make cold calls has no basis. You are just as likely to catch an executive picking up their phone whether you call before work hours or during. If you have a good pitch, and are persistent, you will eventually get to them. You are also just as likely to catch someone in a good mood, or in need of what you have and willing to take your call, on a Monday at 10:00am as you are on a Friday at 2:00pm. The worst thing you can do is relegate your outreach only to certain times. Just pick up the phone or send your emails at all hours you can, and if you really want, track when you got a hold of a person or when they replied, and replicate that. See what works for you.

The one thing that does make a difference is ensuring that when you prospect, set aside a block of time specifically for it. Stay focused, and don't try to do other activities along with it.

Where to focus

The most common way to determine where to put your efforts is to tier your accounts by putting them into categories based on the potential revenue they can generate. That potential is based on criteria relevant to what you're selling. Some do this with a 1-2-3 approach, with 1 being the top accounts to which you do the most strategic outreach since they can produce the largest sales. Accounts in 2 are reserved for lower level email outreach and 3 gets little or no outreach at all. I don't like this approach too much since I've seen a lot of my smaller accounts produce big deals. This was especially true when what I was selling was based on what my product did rather than the number of users the customer has. A marketing team with 2 people can still need a $50,000 marketing solution. But the 1-2-3 approach is a simple and good way to start.

A more strategic way to tier is based on categories. These categories can include accounts that are already customers, accounts using a competitive product you want to target, and accounts in a specific geography. This is better than the first method because in the first method you could put an account in Group 3 because they have a small number of employees, but under the second way, you might recognize that account is using a competitive product that is vulnerable and it could be an easy sale for you. The category method is a lot less arbitrary but also takes more research to learn about them. How you tier is specific to your territory and company, but you'll want some way to attack your accounts.

Once you choose how to tier, you'll want to determine how much time to spend prospecting on all your accounts. Some follow the 80/20 rule where 80% of your time (and thus 80% of sales) comes from prospecting to 20% of your accounts. But I've seen a colleague who had a dozen accounts spend 90% of his time on one that ended up producing a $2 million sale. It was a risky move to put all his eggs in one basket, but he was confident based on everything he knew, and it paid off. Again, this is something each rep needs to decide for what works best in their territory.

Do the research

Before prospecting, it's good to do some research on your accounts to tailor your pitch. I learned to focus on three things: the organizational chart, the strategic plan, and what their competitors are doing. Here's why:

Research	Objective
Organization Chart	Learn who decision makers and their bosses are, and research them before reaching out
Strategic Plan	See where their focus is and ask questions based on that
Competitor Landscape	Find out if they are trying to keep up or doing things differently

The org chart is obvious since it tells you who is in the position you want to contact so you can research them on places like LinkedIn. The strategic plan is helpful but I didn't put much stock in. It's usually done for show to satisfy shareholders or the public. Most companies, at least the smart ones, realize their plan needs to change as the business environment around them changes. But it's still a good document to start a conversation. Lastly, knowing what their competitors are doing is important to understand the context of your industry and ask your customer what they are doing to stay with the competition. These three areas are great places to start to do research to deliver targeted messages when doing your outreach.

The perils of email

If you use email as the primary means for outreach, be ready for curt responses like "not interested" and "take me off your list." I've heard these replies many times and you will, too, so don't let it affect you. That was a mistake I made. When I would get these responses, I would think, how could someone tell me to take them off my list? I was writing from some of the largest and most well-known companies. Did these people realize I was writing from Salesforce, the #1 company in the world for customer management technology? We did $8 billion in sales last year. Schools all over the country are using us! Did I mention I have a six-figure salary? Getting these kinds of replies was a real shock to my ego when I thought I deserved better (which I didn't).

There are many reasons why this happened and why email can be ineffective. Mainly it's because emails are too impersonal. When emailing a prospect, you are putting yourself in the same class as the other marketing spam they get. When you send an email to a customer, no matter how well researched and targeted it is, you are automatically precluding the prospect from ever replying. First, they may never open it. There are tools that let you know if an email has been opened but you can't tell if they read it. It's more likely that the read receipt confirming they opened it was just the result of the person clicking on the message to delete it. Second, it might never even make it to their inbox if their spam filter catches it, but you will not even know.

Emails also take a lot of time to generate and even longer to garner a response, if you get one at all. You can spend 30 minutes carefully crafting an email message before sending it and then have to wait several hours, days, or weeks waiting for a reply. I've had many cases where it's taken 5 emails over the course of a month before a prospect told me they are not interested. A good solution is to shorten your emails to one or two lines referencing a colleague, their strategic plan, or a competitor, and ask for 15 minutes to chat. Short and sweet with a good subject line can save you a lot of time, and provides just as good a chance for a reply as a long, drawn out message.

Writing a lot of emails also took a toll on my health, both physical and mental. To sit and type dozens of messages, on top of all the other emails I was sending, left my back strained and my fingers in pain. There are many days where I've been left crippled from this work. It's also mentally draining. As mentioned, it was deflating to spend all day sending emails to people who had no interest in what I was saying. Getting a reply from someone telling you to take them off your list puts you right up there with a telemarketer. How many times have I received an email to sell me something and replied before finishing the first sentence to take me off their list? I was now that sender. This experience left me asking myself if emailing people to solicit business is what my life has come to. Just the word solicit itself sounds dirty. Think of a "No Soliciting" sign on a business or homeowner's door. No matter what you are selling when you send that email, you are in the same category as a door-to-door vacuum salesman. It's a discouraging realization. You need thick skin to deal with it. Or find a way to prospect from a stronger place.

Pick up the phone

What's the solution to the ineffectiveness of emailing your prospects? The answer is as simple as picking up the phone. That's right, the good old-fashioned phone. It's been around way longer than email and is much more efficient and effective. The problem is most salespeople, myself included, dislike making calls and think it's beneath them. But if you're in sales and are not picking up the phone every day to make calls to prospects, then start today, or consider quitting your job and finding a new line of work. Picking up the phone solves several problems that come with sending emails.

Email is a copout for the scared salesman. It's for someone who's afraid to get rejected by a living, breathing human being so they hide behind a computer. It's like people who would not say to someone's face what they post to social media or the comments section of an article. My recommendation is to welcome the rejection. Seek it out. Find other ways in life to get rejected so you are used to it. Ask someone out on a date. Negotiate price at a farmers' market. Ask for a dollar on the street. If you are not getting rejected, or failing, in your outreach, and in life, then you are not doing enough of it or taking enough risks. Have you seen the movie *Boiler Room* referenced in the beginning of this chapter? If not, then watch it immediately. It should be enough to motivate you to pick up the phone. But watch out as the movie can intimidate some when realizing how ruthless sales can be. For a reminder of the importance of phone calls versus email, this handy table on the next page explains it:

Challenge	Email	Phone
Gatekeepers	Will screen and delete message before it reaches the right person.	Will block you from prospects but can sweet-talk them to get through. Can collect information from them.
Messaging	Lengthy email will not be read. Shorter message makes it difficult to get entire point across.	30-second elevator pitch can get main point across. Might earn you more time. Differentiates yourself. Personal.
Adaptability	One directional. No opportunity to shift message unless you follow-up with another email about another product.	Allows you to change message mid-call if prospect is not interested (important if you offer several products).
Efficiency	Forced to wait days or weeks before prospect replies, if they ever do.	Can find out on the spot if customer is interested and proceed accordingly.
Coverage	Up to 20 emails a day is a lot. Requires a lot of time per message.	Can make 50 or more dials in a day. Takes 10 seconds to reach someone.
Health	Carpal tunnel. Back pain. Headaches.	Easy to dial, more fun, dynamic.

Get someone to do it for you

If you're not calling or emailing, then a good solution is to get someone to do it for you. Hopefully your company has a Business Development Representative (BDR) or similar position that generates leads. It's very effective to have someone make calls where the only objective is to set time to speak with you. No sales, no pressure. The BDR is just asking if the prospect can set aside 15-30 minutes to talk with the salesperson. I've done this myself in reaching out to higher-level executives, who didn't want to talk to a salesperson, and asked them if they would take time to talk with an executive from our company. Reaching out with the goal of connecting the prospect to someone else can really get the sales process going. And when it does get to the salesperson, it's now a warm lead. Don't look at the first call as a time to get the sale. It's only a vehicle to get you to the next step in the process.

If you don't have a BDR, then be your own. Just send an email from your account and tell them this is John Smith writing on behalf of you to ask for time to talk with you. Or create a second email account for your "BDR." Find someone to play the part for you. It's okay to lie. Remember you are in sales. It will not be the first or last time. Besides, it's a petty white lie that's not hurting anyone. Although keep in mind that any lie is still a lie that can catch up to you, especially if the customer asks about the person you fabricated!

Networking and referrals

Whether you're calling or emailing, both can become a waste of time. It's rare that a worthwhile sale is made where the first point of entry is through a cold call, and even less, through a solicitation email. Have you ever bought a home, car, computer, suit, or piece of jewelry after someone emailed or called with a sales pitch? Now how do you think that is going to happen selling, for example, software that costs hundreds of thousands or millions of dollars?

There's a difference between prospecting and networking, and most of the better salespeople I've seen rarely do the former. They focus on reaching out to prospects through a network they've created and let it do the work for them. They get existing customers or other colleagues to make introductions for them. They make one sale and then sell more to other divisions within that account. This way, the process starts out from a place of trust. Think about if you are looking to meet a significant other. Prospecting is approaching them at a bar or dating website. Networking is getting introduced through a mutual friend.

But networking only works if a salesperson does a good job selling to that initial person and they like and trust them enough to make the referral. As you'll learn in Chapter 9, I was not the best at following this approach and rarely got referred to other customers. This was a huge mistake. I would make a sale and then move on to the next prospect on my own.

Prospecting is a one-way street. It's impersonal. And once the sale is made the relationship tends to end. People who network form bonds with their customer and add them to their network to keep producing more leads. Here's the difference:

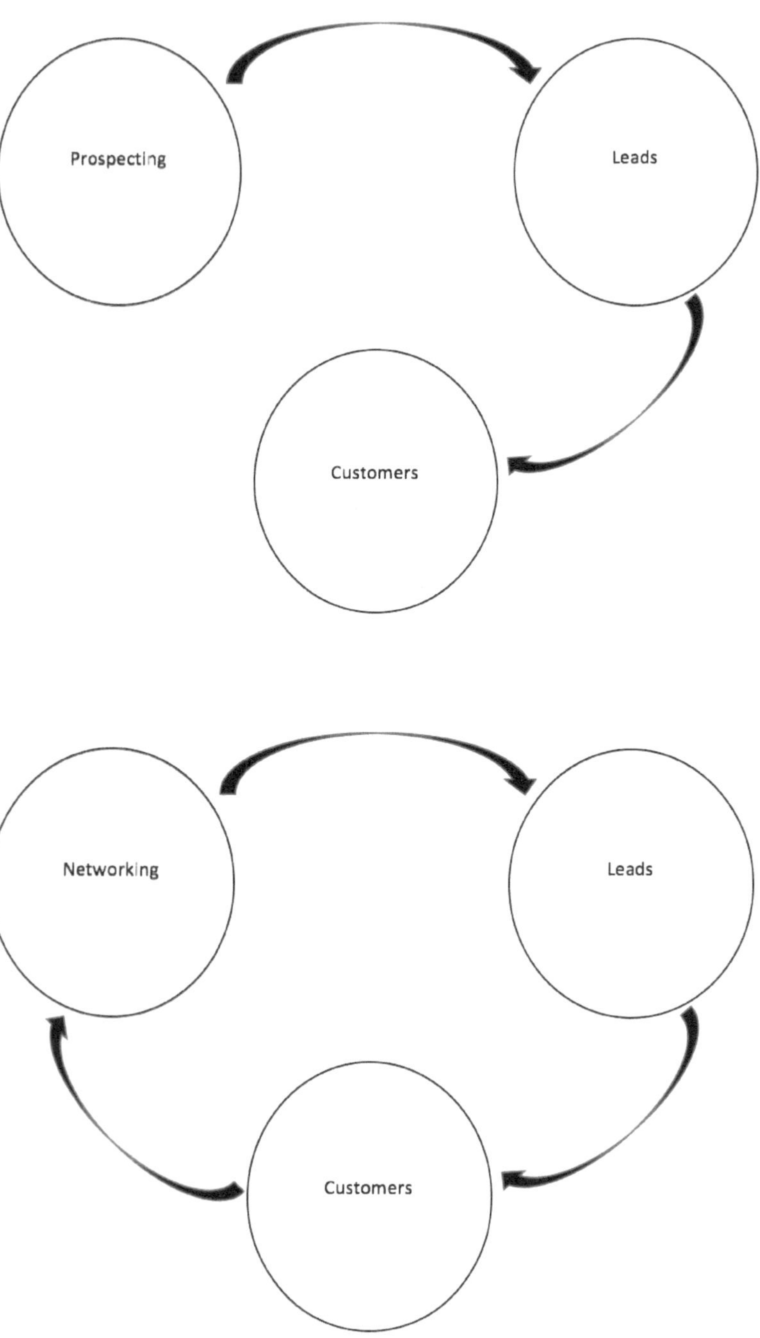
Prospecting
Leads
Customers
Networking
Leads
Customers

Conferences are a great way to build a network. It gives you access to dozens of contacts in a specific setting who are there in part to learn about new solutions for their business challenges. You can meet so many people, even those not at your accounts. You can also get a lot of connections on LinkedIn. Whether you have a base of customers or not, the best way to focus your time finding new business is to create a network and get referrals from those colleagues.

Hustle

With all the different ways to prospect, the one thing to remember is that hustle matters. It goes back to the Vince Lombardi quote from Chapter 2. You'll generate more opportunities through "luck" if you prepare with more outreach. That's when I had the most success. I was knocking on as many doors as I could and stumbled into a lot of sales. You'll get an email reply from an interested prospect if you send 20 emails a day instead of 10. You'll catch a prospect on the phone right before he is leaving work because you were still making calls at 5:30pm. You'll meet the prospect you've been chasing down for months because you attended the conference she is at. It's the same thing as finding a job. You need to send more resumes. It's the same as finding a date. You need to ask more people out. But it's also important to ensure the outreach is as much quality as quantity. Put yourself out there enough and someone will eventually respond. Remember, it's a contact sport.

Advertising

The prolific author and social critic H.G. Wells said that advertising is a form of legalized lying. He understood the false messages that reside in an ad that tries to coerce someone to buy something they didn't know existed and really don't need. As much as I similarly distrust advertising, it can be very effective to get your prospect interested in your product. It's needed to cast a wide net to many people and bring leads to you without you having to do direct outreach. It's also effective because it makes the prospect think they are making the choice to consider your product instead of the salesperson being the one to force the issue. So hopefully the company you are working for is doing corporate marketing.

Seven months into a technology sales job, I had generated little pipeline. I spent countless hours each day writing emails and making calls but just could not get people to reply or buy into my messaging. I was doing everything the company asked me to do and was trying all kinds of methods. It produced some results but not the whale of a deal I needed.

Then I received a lead from a communications manager at one of my largest accounts who called into the company's 800 number. He wanted to learn more about our email-marketing product. He had been searching on the Internet for solutions and happened to be served a web advertisement of our company. It prompted him to call to learn more about the product and how it could be used to send over 13 million emails a year. What also made the lead so stunning was that I would have never thought to reach out to this person. He worked in a small department but happened to be tasked to find the solution for the entire company since he had marketing experience. I could have called and emailed into the account for months (which I had) and never reached out to him since it was so unlikely that he would oversee making such a large purchase. It ended up leading to a $70,000 deal.

Let them come to you

The last story is a good example of why sometimes you shouldn't do any prospecting at all. By prospecting, you are often the one forcing the issue and that is rarely a good way to get someone to do something. If that person really does have a problem that needs solving, then chances are they are going to find you, especially if you work for a good company. I know this contradicts the idea of hustling, but there are times where you need to sit back and let prospects come to you. If you work with your current customers deeply enough they will come to you when it's time to buy more and provide referrals. If your company is advertising properly then there is a better chance leads will come to you. Even better is if your company is hosting webinars, conferences, and other events where you can invite customers and sell without selling.

A balanced approach

As is often the case in life, a balanced approach is the best way to go. To acquire a lot of leads, you should be doing a little bit of everything. There's no hard and fast rule for it but an even split is fair. If my leads were coming from 25% calls, 25% emails, 25% corporate advertising, and 25% customer referrals, I had plenty to work on. The times I got too heavily invested in any single way was when my pool of leads would drain. Diversity is usually good to have in life. It's also helpful to track what sources are producing leads that eventually turn into sales. This way you can invest more or less time into where the good leads are coming from. And don't be static with your messages. Test different ones to see what works. If you send 40 emails in a week, try batches of 10 with different structures to see what garners the most replies. Then replicate that on a larger scale.

RFPs

One last note about prospecting is that you'll also encounter the allure of the Request for Proposal (RFP). RFPs are used when companies have a project they need done and want responses from multiple vendors in a seemingly open competition to win the business. RFPs are exciting because it's like a big present dropped in your lap. I didn't have to do much to get the opportunity (RFPs are often public) and I felt I had just as good a chance as anyone else to win it because RFPs are meant to be objective. There's a clear criterion in the request of how responses will be judged. But RFPs are the siren call of the business development world: a beautiful lead calling you to work it, only to find out that it's a complete time waste where you have no chance of winning.

RFPs are not objective. They are almost always released with a company already in mind that the customer will choose. The customer's interest in buying does not result in an RFP where they really want to see what everyone has to offer. It only results in an RFP because a competitor was already working the deal but now the customer is required by law, or company policy, to go through the RFP process. They need to open it up to public competition and get a certain number of replies to show they tried to get the best price.

A simple heuristic is that if you did not know an RFP was being released until you get the RFP, then don't bother replying. They already know who they are choosing. Instead, try to reach out to the company and ask for a meeting with the decision makers. Often the RFP has rules where questions must be directed to someone from the procurement office that is running the project. If they will not give you access to the actual decision makers then do not waste your time replying to the RFP. It's better to go past them and reach out directly to the likely decision makers. If they refer you back to procurement, and even threaten to disqualify you for reaching out to them, then reach out to them again. It doesn't matter since you have no chance to win it anyway. Better to get disqualified than waste your time. And it will be a lot of time. RFPs are intended to be very long and detailed to weed out companies. There are several cases where I've spent weeks of my time, and the time of others, to reply to an RFP.

Please do not follow my example. If there is one thing I regret about how I prospected, it's replying blindly to an RFP.

On the other hand, if you did have discussions with the decision-makers prior to the RFP being released, then certainly reply, even if you are not certain you will win. One time I called a VP at a small university in Missouri to ask if he was interested in a service I had. He told me that they were about to release an RFP the following day and my company was on the list to send it to. Talk about luck! We spoke for a while and I sold him on our solution before the rule to go through procurement took effect. Even after the RFP was released, the guy took my call and we talked about getting us on the short list of companies they were planning to invite to present in person for the second round of the process. In the end, I had some bad luck when a new Republican governor cut $82 million for higher education from the state budget, $2.2 million of which went to that school, causing them to not move forward with the project.

Prospecting for leads started off as one of my favorite things to do as a salesperson. When I first started in sales as a bright-eyed 22-year-old, I had so much energy to email, pick up the phone, and knock on doors. The problem was that as I got later into my career, this was not as fun. I had a hard time doing that at 36 and felt leads should have been coming to me. I thought prospecting was beneath me, and I didn't like it. But this was the result of my own misguided efforts since I had been hopping from job to job. By staying in one job and industry, you accumulate more contacts and respect in your field, and people will trust you and come to you.

Chapter 5:
Working Decision Makers

Who makes the purchasing decisions in your household?

-A basic consumer survey

Hopefully, your prospecting has paid off and you have a lot of opportunities in your pipeline. A good rule of thumb is to have five times your quota in prospective sales. As these leads come in, now the real work starts of navigating the decision-making process. Before we go into how to do it (and not do it), here is a quick guide of the personas of each type of decision maker that I'll be referring to:

The Point Person

Typically, the first person and main contact you work with throughout the process. They are likely an end-user of the product, which is why you reached out to them first to find out if there's a problem that needs fixing. If they called you it's because they are tasked with being the information gatherer and screening each company. This person can become a gatekeeper who prevents you from reaching the more important people. This is because they start the project wielding a lot of power and they can become reluctant to give it up, so now they hold on to the process as much as they can. Build a relationship with this person and have them get you as far along in the process in the shortest amount of time. But the longer you dabble with them, the more likely you are to spin your wheels with them.

The Talker

The Talker loves to talk but takes little action. They will suggest a course of action, only to replace it with another course of action, so nothing ever gets done. They prefer things to stay exactly where they are despite claiming to be a change agent. They can influence a deal to get stalled and rarely influence it to move forward. But the Talker can be a great way to find out about the challenges to the business, but from there, the salesperson needs to take that challenge directly to someone who will really act. The Talker needs to be tamed. They like power, which needs to be met with power by the salesperson. Challenge the Talker to describe how the change they advocate will get done. They are typically not an end-user of the product and care more about how the product can help the organization than about how the solution technically works.

The Advocate

Unlike the Talker, the Advocate is where the action is. The Advocate not only wants a solution in place, they will actively work to see that the solution they want wins. The Advocate is vocal and strong. They are one person but can have the voice of five. People will often back down from what the Advocate wants because they don't want to deal with them. The problem with the Advocate is that if they are not on board with your product then you will have a difficult time fighting them. If they are on your side, there's also a big down side if the perception of them by others starts to fall apart, which it can since decisions can be very political. As a salesperson, you need to find out who the advocate is and harness their power to your advantage. They are likely an end-user, which is why they want control over the solution they will end up having to use.

The Voter

The Voter is just that – a person who has one vote in the process and quietly casts it for their choice. The Voter can be overlooked by the salesperson who is overly fixated on the other, more obvious personalities, even though the Voters outnumber everyone else. In a project that has 10 decision-makers, the Voter is as many as five of them. Committee decisions are still a numbers game so it's critical to get to the Voters and make sure they are siding with you. The Voter is a great source of information and is someone you can cite to others about what they like about your product and dislike about the competition. They are also an end-user so make sure you are asking a lot of questions about their needs so they see you as caring and understanding them.

The Final Decision Maker

The Final Decision Maker (FDM) is unquestionably the most important person to get to. This is where the power resides. Think of them as the head of the household that no matter what everyone else wants, they make the decision. Usually it's for good reason because it's their reputation and job on the line if things go good or bad. It's also their money as they are the one allocating the budget. By far the FDM is the hardest person to get to. No sale gets made unless the salesperson has direct access to this person, which usually takes an intro from the Point Person or a direct outreach from the salesperson, which I'll go over later in the chapter. The FDM is not an end-user and cares more about cost, implementation, and the return on their investment.

It's important not to confuse the roles of each person described above with their personality types and what they care about. Their role will dictate how you use them to get the sale, but how you are able to use them comes from focusing on their personality types. Personalities vary more than roles and it's not possible to narrow the former down to this book. This is something you should feel out in meetings and relate to each person based on his or her preferences. Some personality types include a person who values personal relationships, technical capabilities, product security, or references from other customers. Find out what each person likes and relate to them as best you can.

Step 1: Determine their objectives

As you work with the different decision makers, you need to understand their objectives. What are their challenges and what needs to be done to overcome them? Without knowing their objectives, you have no idea how to get to your value. Until you know, you are not able to sell anything. You might be able to move the process along but you are bound to hit a roadblock at some point if you can't go back to their compelling reasons to have to buy.

Objectives are tied to features. When I sold floor coatings, the business needed it to have a non-slip surface. When I sold textbooks, the professor needed the book to cover a certain subject in a specific way. When I sold advertising solutions, the media agency needed to be able to measure the performance of the ads. These are all objectives they had and I needed to show them *how* the features of my solution helped them do this. But this is different than the benefits, or the *why*, that my product provided, as we'll see in the next section.

Determining objectives doesn't require a Rolodex of replies to overcome their objections or to provide a solution. During this phase, you shouldn't be making statements about what your product does or selling anything. Just ask as many open-ended questions as you can. Don't talk too much. The initial discovery calls should be the customer talking 90% of the time with you facilitating the conversation and clarifying their answers to ensure you understand what they are saying. Never interrupt! There are few things more frustrating to both a customer and someone else from your company to hear a salesperson jump in as the customer is talking. This means finishing their sentence or starting a question or comment before they are done. It happens all the time. This is not only disrespectful, but worse, it shows you are not paying attention to what they are saying. You are showing your fixation on something they said earlier and trying to reply to that when maybe what they say at the end of their comment is what you really need to listen to. Let them finish, take a pause, and then respond, not react. I know this is hard for myself and many people to pause when in conversation. It's awkward and uncomfortable. But it creates some of the needed tension that I describe in Chapter 6. Life is not an episode of *Law and Order* where everyone knows exactly what to say the split second someone else is done talking. Once I learned to give some room to pause, I found that conversations were understood much better by both parties.

Step 2: Find out their "Why"

If your solution has value, then establishing it should be the easiest part of the sales process. It's simple, but can sometimes be assumed and not explained thoroughly enough because salespeople are focusing too much on features and not connecting it to the benefits. Find out what your customers would use your product for and how their current solution, or lack of one, is holding their business back. Once you do that then ask what their goals are and how the product they need can really help their business. Simply get to the heart of why they need what they need and explain how what you are offering does that. Your value is different from their objectives. The latter is what they want to do, and the former is the result your product will bring.

Here's an example. I reached out to a graduate school of business at a major university in Texas. They were struggling to connect with businesses outside of their typical geographical region and needed to do so to increase enrollment of their programs. Oil prices were dropping and as a result, the industry was shedding jobs. Their market for students was shrinking as fewer people could afford the cost of continuing their education. They needed a tool to help them manage outreach to a larger number of businesses to see if they would refer their employees to the school.

I discovered all of this in one call by asking a few basic questions. I talked about how the technology I was selling allowed them to create accounts, contacts, track activities, take notes, and communicate with internal colleagues. I showed how they can set reminders for follow up and store emails into the system with the click of a button from their Gmail and Outlook accounts. These were all the objectives they had and wanted in a solution.

But all the functionality my product offered was not the value. My value was that I made their job easier. I made them more efficient. I could help them increase enrollment, which increased revenue. This made them look better to their superiors and helped advance their careers. It wasn't just the first level features that drove this sale, it was tying how all of it made them and their business more successful. That is value. By the time I got to price, there was barely a murmur of it being too expensive (it was way more than the competition) because I had already showed them how their investment was going to generate a return. I had something to fall back on had they complained about price.

Going back to the last section, here are the differences between the features and benefits of what I sold:

Solution	Features	Benefits
High quality floor coating	Non-slip, looks better	Safe workers, compliance
Preferred textbook	Covers what professor can't teach in class	Allows them to teach more difficult topics in class
Ad delivery platform	Can display any ad on any site	Provide analytics on ad effectiveness to keep client and revenue

Smart people make a purchase based on value, and good salespeople drive the value of what they are selling more than just what it does.

Step 3: Confirm budget and timing

In Chapter 7 I'll discuss negotiating price, which occurs after you've properly scoped your customer's needs and you've established your value. When it's still early in the sales process, you want to focus on their budget, not your cost. It's an important distinction. When you start the sale, you need to be the one to control the budget discussion. The salesperson needs to ask who owns the budget, how much they've allocated to the project, and how they will get additional funds if the project goes over. The customer may not have all the answers and that's fine. Or they might give you a number that is below what your solution costs. That's fine, too, since budget can go up as a customer is more sold on your solution being the right one. Whatever their answers, it gives you a good indication of how to proceed and what you need to find out.

If the customer asks you how much your solution is, now it becomes a pricing discussion. You are on the defensive, having to deflect the question by telling them you don't know enough about their needs to provide an accurate cost. It may be true but now the customer might become a little uneasy. They can get anxious to hear a price and if you don't give an answer it might make them think you are hiding something. If they press you harder then give them a wide range where the high end will certainly exceed what they'd end up paying. But if you can set expectations from the start of what you need to know before you can provide an accurate cost, that will help push this question back to the point where they sold on your solution.

A key way to drive the value of your product for when you eventually get to your price is to talk about their return on investment (ROI). This comes from finding out their objectives and why they want to buy. When I sold marketing solutions to higher education, their objective was to enroll more students, so I worked to establish how my service would do that. If I could show them how a $50,000 yearly marketing solution would bring them 200 new students a year, who each generated $1,000 of profit a year, they could see that $50,000 would bring them a return of $200,000. Sometimes the case is not as clear-cut, especially if their need is to increase efficiency or something that is non-quantitative. In these cases, I wanted to find out how much time their employees could save to put towards other responsibilities and quantify that. For example, making the case that a marketing solution can automate their ad campaigns, which means they wouldn't need to hire a full-time person whose cost would well exceed what I was offering.

If a customer thinks your solution is the best but your price is too high, this is a good situation. But it requires work to continue establishing your value. ROI is a great way to do this. Another way is to think back to the example in Chapter 1 when I was selling the floor to Sauk Machine Works. They were going to invest in a critical part of their infrastructure yet the owner was trying to save a few bucks to do it. He needed to be challenged as to how much cheaper it would be to pay more now to do it right than to have to make repairs in the future. This way of thinking should apply to every purchase people make. Pay good money up front for high-quality items, and you'll pay less in the long run. Think about a desk you purchase from Wal-Mart. It might only cost $100 but chances are it is cheap material, it will not assemble correctly, and six months later you'll dislike it and want to buy a new one. It's the high cost of buying cheap. Put up the extra $100-$200 at the start and buy a high-quality desk you'll like for years.

Ensuring that you understand your customer's overall timing to implement the solution will also help drive the budgeting discussion. If they tell you they can't go live for six months and you ask why, they might tell you that's when their new fiscal year starts. You might also find out they need to release an RFP before they can buy and that process takes 3 months. By finding out their timing, you can build an implementation schedule so they see the path it will take to get to their end goal. Timeline also helps the salesperson to follow up in proper time intervals and to know when to expect the business to close so they can forecast for their quota.

Forget your PowerPoint

When doing discovery calls and moving the process forward, sales people often turn to PowerPoint slides to deliver their message. Like the warmth of a mother's hug, the PPT makes salespeople feel secure that everything will be okay. I always felt so much better if I had some slides to turn to. It gave the meeting a quantitative aspect so I knew exactly where it would go. The PPT could speak for me and I could speak to it. It was that extra person I brought to the call to support me and to let attendees know I prepared ahead of time with some great slides. This was rubbish. The PPT was a crutch when both of my legs were working just fine.

Much like forcing the process to get to a demo or proposal (which I'll explain later), making a PPT directs the process in a way where it might not naturally go. It tries to control the uncontrollable. Sales is a fluid, evolving process, and each meeting is a microcosm of that. To come in with slides that dictate what you will talk about predetermines everything. It boxes in the salesperson. Of course, you need to prepare and have talking points ready, but to shape this into slides is not always necessary.

Take the corporate history I would talk about with customers when working with Salesforce. We had a few slides that told the story of who we are. The first showed the awards Salesforce has received and the next illustrated our past growth and where we were headed. Then the next two talked about the community service work we were doing.

When talking about this, I would wonder why we were told to do it through slides. I was trying to tell my customers who we were and about our values. I was trying to personalize it. But when I talk to someone in my personal life about who I am, do I pull slides to show my recent increases in money given to the homeless? Or show a chart that illustrates my evolution from a transactional salesperson to someone working on larger enterprise deals? No, I just talk like a regular person. The more I could do this in sales calls and talk in a natural way, the more I was able to really connect with my customers. I found it much easier and better received to tell an honest story of a volunteering experience I did that Salesforce initiated.

Know the politics

The personal likes and dislikes of your decision makers towards each other and towards the salesperson can play a bigger factor in who they vote for than the product itself. I once had a customer who was Egyptian tell me he was voting for, "The Brown Book," the title he gave my product which was called, *The Little Brown Handbook*, an English grammar text I was selling to his department. He didn't even know the title of the book but was voting for me strictly because he liked me and my skin was as dark as his. But spite can play an equal part as I've seen people vote against others and me simply because of their dislike. Think of political elections: often, people don't vote based on a candidate's policies as much as because they like their candidate or dislike the other candidate.

This can extend to the politics of your company. Using Salesforce again as an example, they are a liberal company that takes an active role in working to shape the political climate of our country. From equal pay for women to not discriminating against people, their CEO lets his voice be heard. There's no doubt that stances like this can rub some people the wrong way and make them not want to work with you because of that. This works on the other side of the political aisle as well, but is not meant to say that companies should not express a political view. Sometimes your beliefs are more important than money.

How are they deciding?

It's important to know how the decision makers are coming together to make the decision. There are many ways including a one-person, one-vote committee decision. In these cases, it's as important to work the Voter as it is the FDM. Although what the latter wants can sway how everyone else votes and not so much the other way around. In this situation, you need to know who each is voting for and count your totals. Don't be afraid to ask each person for their vote. It doesn't have to be a private vote where people might feel it's none of your business since in this case it is directly your business. You may not get a straight answer but you at least need to ask or know based on what they are telling you.

Another process to make a decision involves an open discussion where a solution is picked by general consensus. This typically happens when the group meets after they've reviewed all potential solutions and talk it out to pick a winner. These meetings have more of an unknown factor. You might think it's yours to win going into that meeting but then someone speaks up for another solution and sways everyone else. This is when getting to the Advocate and the Talker is critical so they speak up for you.

The most likely process for a decision is when the person at the top makes the decision with input from a few people. This makes the most sense since it's that person that owns the success of the project and the budget. It's their neck on the line that what they choose is the right solution. This is my favorite situation because it shows real leadership. I also like this situation because it's clear as to who you need to get to. You know who makes the decision in the household and you can go right to that person. It's also the most difficult because if you don't have that person favoring your solution or can't get to them, it's less likely you will win. But this also means you know where you stand. If you don't have that person on your side, you can walk away and save yourself the time and effort of fighting an uphill battle. It also means you can take more risks to try to overcome those hurdles since you know it's likely you will not win the deal anyway.

The silo

The one thing you should not do above all else is silo your decision makers. What that means is, do not work with decision makers where they are figuratively speaking in a silo by themselves while the other decision makers are in another silo or nowhere to be found at all. It is the most detrimental thing to blocking you from getting a sale.

The silo is so harmful because you can flawlessly execute on all the key areas of the sales process, but if you are not selling to the right decision makers it makes no difference. It's the same in any sales situation. If I go to buy a car and the salesman works me perfectly, but my wife who is at work makes the decision with me, a sale will not be made. It's important for the salesman to find out as early as possible who is making the decision, how it will be made, and proceed accordingly.

The silo is also harmful because it disjoints the information you are providing and who you are providing it to. I can tell the same thing to five different people but chances are they will understand it differently and share it with others that way. The more you can provide information to the whole group the easier it is to make sure everyone is on the same page and to answer all their questions more effectively. It also saves time to not have to repeat things several times. A simple way to do this is to copy everyone on the emails you are sending. Or if someone asks you a question make sure you let everyone know the answer, since they might have that same question. Keeping communication to the whole group as much as possible also lets you know what the team needs and not just each individual person.

There is a time to silo decision makers when politics might dictate you extract information from one person to take it to another. Sometimes you need a little insider information to sway the committee or another person. The dynamics of the process will dictate when and how this is appropriate.

Get to the FDM

Your goal with working the decision makers is to get to the person(s) with the power to make the decision. Who those people are needs to be addressed early. On a first call, if the Point Person tells me the CFO makes the final decision, a meeting with the CFO better be part of the next steps. If the initial gatekeeper tells you to work through her only, I immediately figure out how I will approach the CFO since I know the sale will not be made unless I get access to them. If this happens, it happens naturally. If you are positioned to get the sale, the people you are working with will get you to the FDM. It just takes persistence and a good selling methodology to get them to trust you. When that time comes, it might help to get someone higher-level at your company with you on the meeting so power can speak to power. Just remember in the meantime to balance your time among all the other decision makers who will be easier to get to.

It's easy to get into situations where you are in a silo with one or a few of the decision-makers and can't get to the FDM. It's easy because often a salesperson starts the process by contacting a mid-level decision-maker. An FDM or other high-level person may not take your call, or isn't involved with the initial vetting, so you talk to the mid-level contact to gather information. This is normal but also why it's so important to ensure it doesn't continue. The longer you go not getting to the FDM, the harder it will be to get there. Nothing is worse than having a couple of calls with your initial contact and empowering them only to then ask who else you need to talk to. It makes you look timid that you didn't ask earlier but wanted to, or incompetent for not knowing to ask earlier. It might also threaten them by making them feel less important, or worry them because it's their boss they are introducing you to. Additionally, the more information you give them, the more difficult it is for them to relay it all accurately to others.

You can pretty much assume the decision by a business to make a purchase is made by more than one person, especially for any complex sale (a transactional, A to B sale is different since there really might only one person involved). A simple heuristic is that if you are only working with one person in the process you are missing something. I wish I had followed this obvious notion when I was working with the technology company Blackboard, and along came Fort Hays State University.

FHSU called me as they were interested in purchasing Blackboard's call center support to handle after-hours technology requests made by students and faculty. FHSU was already a Blackboard customer so it made sense to expand the relationship. At first, everything was great as the guy who called was from the same country as my parents. We talked about personal things and our families and got to know each other well. Over the ensuing weeks, we outlined a solution that was just right for them. As we were working together, I asked several times if we could get his boss and the FDM, who was the Chief Information Officer, on the phone. He kept saying not to worry about him and promised me he had the power to decide along with a couple of Voters he had on our calls. After some negotiation on price, he promised me that if I could get my final cost under a specific number, the deal was mine. After much discussion internally with Blackboard, I got him the price he wanted.

What happened next is obvious looking back on it. He told me they couldn't move forward and needed more time. He promised me they would buy but at the current time they couldn't find budget in what was the middle of the fiscal year. They needed to wait until the next fiscal year to get the funds. While that turned out to be true, and it's a valid reason to have to wait, that is not the point. The point is that when he asked for the final price cut, I could have used that leverage to ask for something back. I could have told him I need to speak to the CIO before I can reduce the price. If he said no, then I should have told him I'm sorry but I can't proceed until I talk to him to get some assurance the deal will happen. It made me look ridiculous to go to my team at Blackboard and tell them the deal was ours if we could get the price concession and then not get it. But I had no one to blame but myself for not doing what any salesperson needs to do and get access to the right people.

Fort Hays eventually did make the purchase several months later when the new fiscal year started. This was just six weeks after I had left the company. This is another example of luck and circumstance. This account was taken from me after the deal fell through since Blackboard restructured territories among all the sales reps. I was having a tough year and desperate for a sale, and had I not lost that account and got that deal, I would not have left and might still be working at Blackboard.

Go over their head

It's obviously not ideal when you're stuck with the Point Person or someone else. This situation is likely just a symptom of something else you are lacking in the process but it's going to happen in some cases. When it does, I advocate going over the head of the person you are working with and reach out directly to who you need to. You don't have anything to lose since you are not going to get the deal anyway without access to them. When you do reach out, make sure it's at the point when you have enough information to interest them and it's the right timing for a discussion. If it's too early, you risk your one chance to talk as they refer you back to your original contact, who might now be upset with you. If it's too late, their decision will have already been made.

Putting decision makers in a silo happened to me at Rice University when I was working with their School of Continuing Education as they evaluated email tools to market their programs. I visited with the decision makers and did a solid demo with my manager and technology specialist. The marketing team really liked our solution and wanted to pursue it further as they were evaluating other companies. Upon returning to the office, I was following up with the Point Person who was facilitating all the conversations. Our next step was to have another call with the marketing team to discuss pricing, implementation, and other logistical concerns. But as the days and weeks passed, the main contact was slow to reply to my emails and she wasn't returning my calls. When she did reply, it was a message pushing me off for another few days. I was starting to get concerned as we were approaching the date when they said they'd be deciding, and we still hadn't had the pricing call. I felt something was wrong but rather than reach out to the marketing team, I kept working through the main contact. Soon after, I woke up one morning to an email telling me they had decided on another company.

It was my lack of having any relationship with the marketing team that was the real problem. I had a great opportunity when I was on campus for the demo to establish contact with them beyond the meeting. I could have had the Point Person commit to a day and time for the follow-up call. And of course, I could have just emailed the marketing folks and asked for a time to talk. Or at least copied them on an email to the main contact instead of putting her in a silo. If she got upset, I could have told her I thought she said it was okay or that I thought it was the best thing to do. Just play dumb. But instead I trusted her to do the work for me and as time slipped by it became too late for me to do anything, and in the end, the deal was lost.

Working the decision makers is where art and skill become more important. I equate it to a poker tournament, where, like a bunch of sales leads, anyone can get lucky early and acquire chips, but keeping them and accumulating more is the real challenge. It takes real art and skill to maneuver through the field. It takes patience and the ability to read people. Without proper maneuvering and showing strength, it will be tough to ask for what you need to move the process along, and win the whole thing.

Chapter 6: Don't Rush to Demo

*A thousand examples may not prove something,
but one example can disprove it.*

-Antifragile, by Nassim Taleb

At some point during the sales process, the prospect will want to see your solution. After all the questions qualifying their needs and all the talk about what you can do for them, you'll eventually have to show your cards. This typically happens through a demonstration, or demo. A meeting will be called where the decision makers huddle in a room to watch you and your team show them what you've got. The demo is obviously important not only because you can show why your solution is so great and better than the competition, but because it can also advance the sale a big step to getting it closed.

The demo is also unique because it's tangible. There's a specific meeting for it. You can see a demo, hear it, and often, touch it. The demo deserves a lot of attention so it's not surprising how many books there are providing tips and tricks for doing it in the best way. Peter Cohan's, *Great Demo!* instructs salespeople to do the last thing first, meaning show the most compelling part of the solution at the beginning. It grabs the audience's attention, allowing you to work backwards to show everything else. In *Product Demos that Sell,* author Steli Efti advises to sell the demo as much as you sell your solution. Make sure the prospect understands why the demo is important so they show up prepared. Lastly, one point from Rob Falcone's *Just F*ing Demo!* is to speak in your customer's language, not yours. All these suggestions are helpful when it comes time to demo.

The one piece of advice these books are missing is that you shouldn't be in a hurry to demo, or better yet, if you can help it, why you should not demo at all in the traditional way it's done. By not demoing you have more flexibility in approaching the sales process. This advice might sound confusing or ridiculous. If what is being sold is great, how can demonstrating it be a bad thing? How else is a customer going to see how good it is and decide if they like it? As consumers, people need to test drive a car, see a house, or try on a suit before they are ready to buy. Wouldn't any customer expect the same thing when they are thinking of buying what you are selling?

A demo is not an inherently bad thing to always avoid. There's a time and place for it based on each situation. But the way salespeople conduct the demo is often done in an environment that may not be the best to effectively sell their product. The traditional way of demoing where you stand in front of the decision makers as they scrutinize your product is fraught with the possibility that it can hurt more than help. There are better ways to do it but salespeople can be anxious to get to the demo because they believe if they just show a prospect how great their product is, they will buy. This thinking is loaded with misconceptions.

Why a demo?

Before going anywhere near a demo, an understanding is needed of what the customer wants and how a demo will help them decide. It must be qualified. We reviewed in Chapter 5 all the key areas to ensure you've covered by this point. A good example of when not having this information made a demo ineffective was for an opportunity I had with a large account that was reviewing email automation tools. The person running the project was from the IT department and called me to ask if we could host a demo. I was glad to do it but asked to have a scoping call before to better understand the situation. The conversation went like this:

Me: What are the main goals you want to accomplish with this solution?

Prospect: We want to be able to email all the people we interact with and track whether they have opened the emails and took any action with it.

Me: Great, who will be sending the emails for your team? And who will they be going to? Also, what is the purpose of the emails?

Prospect: Those are good questions that we are still determining. The committee is made up of many business units and they want to know what the tool can do first to understand how it will fit into their operations.

Me: Understood. I work with other customers who approach it the same way. Can we first have a call with each business unit to learn more about their strategy? I've found this really helps to effectively show how our solution works and aligns with your needs.

Prospect: I don't think so. The IT department has been tasked with setting up the initial demos to screen each company, and from there, we will select certain ones to go deeper with our teams.

Me: Okay. How much budget has been allocated for this project so I can ensure we are proposing an appropriate solution?

Prospect: The amount of budget we have hasn't been determined yet and we will base that on how much each vendor is proposing.

Me: What is the time-frame you are anticipating the solution will be implemented?

Prospect: We haven't decided exactly when. Likely sometime next year.

Me: Who are the main decision makers who will own the success of this project?

Prospect: It will be made up of several people across the different business units. We'll identify them as we get further along.

Me: How will the demo help you decide on a solution?

Prospect: We are hoping that by seeing its capabilities, we can understand how to form our needs around it.

So here we have a project with no defined strategy or criteria for evaluation, no budget, no firm date as to when it needs to be implemented, and no one owning the project to ensure it happens. They just wanted a demo because they were bored, I guess. But I had no idea how to tailor it to what their specific needs were. I could have done a general demo but that's not going to wow anyone.

I didn't want to do the demo but I no backbone to tell them I couldn't do one until these questions are answered. I still did the demo and sure enough, it didn't go well. We were getting tons of questions from the security team that we were unable to answer. We looked weak having to hesitate when replying and saying that we will check and get back to them. Had we known the questions going into the demo we would have been ready to show them how we can meet their needs. Any demo can lead to questions you can't answer on the spot, but we could have minimized it and provided expectations had we spoken with them first. We also left the room still not knowing enough about their strategy to help put our value against their needs to advance the deal. I'll come back to this story later in the chapter about what I should have done when the prospect first called.

Assuming you have the information you need prior to the demo, you also need to understand why a demo is required. The simple answer is that your customers want to see the solution. But is a demo the only way this can be done? If they request a demo does this mean you must do it or can you direct them to another course of action? And if you do it, how will a demo help them make a final decision? Why a demo can be such a mistake is that salespeople often conduct one when they don't have a clear understanding of what it will accomplish.

Why no demo

It's important to know what problems can arise when you demo to minimize the chances of them happening. There's a lot so for the following reasons you might try to steer them away from the traditional demo:

One directional

A demo is mainly one directional. The structure is you and your team standing in the front of the room with your customers sitting down. It's you talking and them listening. It's you showing your solution with them watching. It's basically the opposite of everything you've done up to this point, which is hopefully more listening than selling. This structure seems to put the salesperson in a situation of power when really, they are in a fragile state. Usually the committee is composed of people with different agendas. What happens if you don't have enough time to show everything to everyone? What happens when you show something that someone else doesn't care about and they get on their cell phone, stare out the window, or start talking to someone else and distract others? What if one person doesn't like what they see and makes it known to everyone else, causing hesitation to accept your product?

A way to minimize these stressors is for a salesperson to do several mini demos to each person or group of people with shared interests, rather than to a larger team. You can go deeper with each group. This takes more time but is worth it. Your prospects will see the value of it and appreciate that you are putting in the time to ensure everyone's needs are met. You can also address any problems your solution has before the prospect shares it with the rest of the group. By the time you get to the group meeting, everyone has seen what they want and can evaluate your solution more effectively.

Negative asymmetry

Another problem with the traditional demo is that there is too much that can go wrong to hurt your chances to make the sale and little that can go right to close it. There's more downside than upside. I've been in countless demos where there was a technical glitch that slowed things down. Whether it was the Internet connection, computer hookups, or something went wrong with what we were showing; anything that made the product look subject to technical difficulties, destroyed my chances. And it doesn't matter if it was my fault or not, or the fact that all technology can go down, because your customer is left with the perception that the solution can't be trusted. This is magnified when it happens in front of all the decision makers. Additionally, what if you are late to the demo or a key decision maker ends up not being able to attend? There goes your one shot to make a good impression. Lastly, if there was one question you can't answer or one thing that came up which you don't have or can't show, once again it hinders your chances.

This happened to me in a demo I did at Rice University for a solution to help them register their students for their courses. The room was filled with 20 people, each with their own needs. A few of them were from the finance team and wanted to know how our solution processed payments. In run-up to the demo, we knew we were not able to show this because it required a high level of customization that we couldn't do in time for the demo. The committee knew that but the people who wanted to see it were nevertheless skeptical that we could deliver and let the room know their feelings. Had I done the demo again, I would have asked them not to come and found a different way to showcase that we could meet their needs. Or not done the demo at all until we were ready to show what those Advocates needed to see.

On the flip side, there were few demos I was a part of where the product portion of it moved the needle in my favor when it wasn't there already. The best you can hope for is that it's a good opportunity to further develop relationships with everyone. There were fewer times when a demo sealed the deal when I not was going to close it anyway. In those cases, a large group demo only hurt my chances. Often, the small differences in product from the competition played no decisive factor. At best, it was a minor incremental step in the right direction that was outweighed by all the other factors such as the relationship and price. If you're choosing between comparable models of a BMW and Mercedes Benz, or a Ford and Chevy, is a test drive really going to make a difference? Probably not, as the competitors are pretty comparable, and it's more a matter of which brand you feel better about.

Can't substitute for the real thing

People expect a demo when they buy anything, whether it's a car, home, or suit. But even in these cases, a demo only gives a false sense of the product's capabilities. You really have no idea if you are going to like what you've bought until you start using it. How often does someone buy a car after a test drive, only to realize it doesn't handle well in the rain? You might realize the house you thought you loved when you toured it is now a nightmare because you have two neighbors with dogs that bark all day. I've paid big money for a Hugo Boss suit I tried on, only to find the stitching came undone after a few months.

Whether it's a product or service, there is a level of faith involved to make these purchases that a demo can't replace. The inherent risk of not liking what you've bought is why CarMax has a 5-day guarantee where you can return a car with no questions asked. It's why people like to shop at Nordstrom because they know they can return something they don't like well after the 30-day return policy. It's why people who buy a home get a yearlong warranty to take care of problems they didn't know about when they bought it. Your customer may not have that option with your product and a demo provides no assurance that what you are selling is something they will be happy with. A demo is even worse because since you're the one showing it, it's equivalent to watching someone else try on a suit and deciding if you want to buy it!

Your customers will appreciate if you are upfront with them and explain that a demo is not their best path to evaluate your solution. Demoing can't replicate how the prospect will really end up using the product, which is why I used the quote in the opening of this chapter. You can do demo after demo, but it might not be enough to prove why your product is the best. But one problem proves it's not the best.

What to do instead

Demos are a great way to advance the sales process, if it's done strategically. First, as a salesperson you should not be suggesting hosting a demo. If a customer requests you do a demo that's fine. That's a good sign they are interested in buying and you can work with them accordingly. But when a salesperson suggests a demo it shows they have nowhere else to take the sale. Why do a demo when you can keep asking questions to discover more about the customer's needs, build the relationship, and establish value? It's a clear case of addition by subtraction. Perhaps the customer is open to buying without ever seeing a demo. Here are some strategies you can do instead:

Pilot

I think about how much more effective I could have been had I got my prospects to use my product before deciding to buy. Had they done so they could have truly understood its capabilities and if it was the right solution. They could then ask me questions about how to use it based on what they were looking for. It requires them to act. It's true that this can cause them to be turned off if they didn't like it. Most salespeople prefer the smoke and mirrors of a demo because it allows them to control what is shown and put it in the best light. But if you really have a great product, this will not happen with a pilot. By doing this you also bring out into the open what they might not like and lets you address it and then compare how the competition works. Someone who is not afraid to lose takes this course of action. They are happy if issues come up rather than sell something the customer later realizes they do not like, and in the long run, does not recommend your product or buy more.

If you must demo, you might be better off setting them up for a pilot or test drive to use it as close to how they would for real. This also invests the customer more into your product since they've taken more time to use it and inclines them to buy it after that. If I got a professor to pilot a homework technology for a small class before using it in his bigger course, it makes him more assured to know what he is using. But I was always in a hurry to shove a demo in my customers' faces, and expect to wow them. It was also what they wanted to do to check the box on their list of criteria they were using to decide. This is the traditional way it's done and people feel comfortable doing it that way. But looking back, I lament at how much more I could have accomplished if I had them test my solution rather than have me show it to them.

I love technology companies that offer 30-day trials or free versions of their software. One example is SurveyMonkey. They have a great tool that allows you to set up free surveys. But if you want to use their advanced features, like including more than 10 questions or customizing your web link, then you pay. As a customer, it allows me to use their product for free, see if I like it, and then pay for the extra level functionality that I now need to make the best survey possible.

Referrals

A great substitute for a demo is to connect your prospect with a satisfied customer. The reference can assure the prospect that you have a great product they are currently happy with. How frequently do you go to sources like Yelp or Amazon to read reviews of a restaurant or product? Getting a current customer who your prospect considers a colleague works wonders. Nothing can demo your product better than another customer confirming it for you. You'll also make a connection between the prospect and the current customer that the former will remember and appreciate. That's how you demo your product. Trust, built through these kinds of relationships, are far more effective. Think about basic word of mouth advertising. We are all way more likely to buy something if a friend told us how much they love it than if a salesman knocks on our door and promises us happiness.

Videos

Demoing also requires a lot of time preparing for it when that time can be spent in better ways, like generating new leads and selling. This is especially true if a salesperson doesn't have a technical support person since they will end up doing the demo on their own. And demoing is not often a skill set for a salesperson and it's very possible the demo will not go well. If a salesperson does have an engineer or technology specialist who does the demo, they might not do it any better, and it also takes several hours of their time they could be spending on other deals.

Another solution is to send your prospect a video of your product that can serve as the demo. If you don't have one then record one killer demo and use that with others. It will save you a lot of time and give you a clue of how interested a customer really is if they watched it. Give them a worksheet to fill out while they do it. Once again, getting them to take action invests them more into your solution.

Create tension

Have you ever worked to attract another person you were interested in romantically? In doing so, have you tried to not do anything that might upset or offend the person for fear it would turn them off and they wouldn't like you? When you did play nice, how often were you successful in your goal? For me, I know the answer is seldom. I know it takes some tension to attract another person. You have to be able to stand up for yourself and your beliefs or the person is going to view you as weak, and be uninterested. If the person says something you find offensive, you have to be able to call them out. Not just because it will end up making you more attractive but also because it means you know what you want and you are not willing to compromise on your values.

This is very much like sales. Often, we are trying to cater to the customer and we don't want to do anything they might find offensive. It's like fearing to press your main contact to get them to introduce you to the final decision maker because it could offend or threaten them. The same goes for when the customer asks you to demo your solution. Just because a customer asks you for a demo doesn't mean you should do it. In the example I gave earlier in the chapter with the email automation tool, what a strong salesperson says is something like this:

"Prospect, I'm excited to hear you have interest in our solution and I'd love to demo how it will meet the needs of your team and the entire organization. The problem is we don't have answers to some of the initial questions that we need to ensure we can demo this properly so you can make an informed decision about whether you want to go further with us. We offer a range of solutions that vary in price, so without knowing your budget, I am not sure what product to propose. I will also not be able to get the internal resources I need to host a demo based on the info I have today. When do you think you'll know more so we can move forward?"

You can use whatever cadence you deem appropriate, but the point is that you must push back a little on your customer. Chances are they will not decide based on what they've told you and you'll waste a lot time for a demo that will not be done effectively. If you push back and the client is offended, then good. No sale has ever been made that didn't have a little friction at some point. If they tell you they will not work under your terms, then forget them. They should be happy that you are guiding them on what they need to do and not wasting their time. I'd much rather step away from a deal with my integrity intact than demo something just to demo it when I know it will hurt more than it will help to get the sale. Walking away is something I should have learned from my days at Thermal-Chem, as I mentioned in Chapter 1.

Another example of the need to create tension is with a university in Missouri, when I spoke with them about a social media-monitoring tool I was selling. The school had just been exposed for conducting animal testing on its campus and got attacked on Twitter with over 10,000 negative tweets that hurt its brand. They realized how fragile they were to social media, so they were searching for a tool that would let them get their message out before the public did to get in front of the next crisis. It was a serious problem that needed a solution quickly (I'll talk about creating urgency in the next chapter).

I had a discovery call with the social media marketers and gathered a lot of information. The next step was a demo, but before that, we needed to qualify their budget and who the FDM was. They promised me their boss had set aside the budget they needed and that it was up to them to decide what to purchase. I requested that the boss be on the demo since I knew if he was the one paying for it he needed to see it and be sold to. But the marketers told me their boss would take their final recommendation and didn't need to be involved. After pressing a little more and not getting them to commit to having their boss join the call, I told them we could still proceed with the demo. After that, I hid behind email with a more forward message telling them we would not do the demo unless their boss was on.

I didn't go through with the demo knowing we would not get the deal unless the boss was on. But I was not happy that I said this through email and not on the call. If I had stood up for myself and what I wanted, I would have told them very politely that I appreciate their desire to evaluate my product, but based on my experience, the boss needs to be on the call to make the sale. It happens many times when we present to the users but the person with the budget doesn't want to pay without knowing more about the product. I should have told him without access to him we can't proceed. It might have offended them, but who cares? I know I'm not going to get the sale without getting the boss involved. If I must create a little tension to get there, that is all part of the game. If they are serious about buying they will get him on the call. After that I ended up reaching back out to host the demo because I panicked.

They never replied and I went out in a weaker position than if I just stuck to my principles from the start. I should have just gone over their heads and reached out to the boss directly.

Demo at the right time

The timing of when to do the demo in relation to the competition is also important. This is especially true if you can't find a differentiator between your product and theirs. To overcome this, you want to present last. This way you can talk to the decision makers after each demo and find out how it went and what they liked and didn't like. Then you can use information as your differentiator to tailor your demo even more to their needs.

Demoing last is also best because it's closer to when the decision will be made. If you go too early, then you can lose momentum, and your customer can forget about your product. You can also learn something after the demo that you could have used. But you will only have one shot to do it. If the competition demos after you, then it's more likely the customer will remember their product more than yours, and they will be the one using information as the differentiator.

As important as the demo seems, it isn't. Most people have their minds made up to buy something even before they see it, and will overlook its shortcomings because they are so fixated on buying. This is because others have it or that person thinks they need it so badly they will not stop until they do. When the perception is that a product or service is good, they don't need the demo to prove it. Does driving a BMW make it a great car, or was it already one before you got in it? Do people buy a Mac because it's the best, or because they perceived it was prior to going shopping? Do people move to Austin, TX because they visited for a few days, or because everyone says how great of a town it is? In these cases, it's the latter reason. Additionally, when a product is good and carries that perception with it, the people selling it don't want to demo it. They know it's good and if you don't then they don't worry about it. I think this is why so many of the solutions engineers I worked with, whose job it was to demo, disliked doing them more than any other responsibility they had.

A live demo presented traditionally needs to be done very strategically and with the utmost caution. There's a time and place for it. Just be aware of why you are doing it, and ensure it's really helping you, and not just something you should do.

Chapter 7: Price, Budget, & Value

Yet unless the exchange be in love and kindly justice,
it will lead but some to greed and others to hunger.

-From Kahlil Gibran's poem, *Buying and Selling*

By the time I would get to discussing price with the prospect, to varying degrees of success I would have followed the path outlined so far in this book in a somewhat linear fashion. If I did a good job, the prospect would be interested in buying, and now it's time to negotiate a price.

In Chapter 5 I talked about the need to determine your prospect's budget and explained the difference between confirming their budget and discussing your price. Hopefully you've done the former at the beginning of the process to know if you should ever move forward. In many cases, I spent a lot of time selling my product only to get far along and realize my customer could not afford it.

Discussing price is done closer to when the customer is ready to buy and after you've covered all the bases. The reason you wait to discuss price is because if you do it too early, it's all your prospect will focus on, and you can find yourself playing catch up as they've lost interest in your solution. It's imperative that once you start talking price, you can fall back on all the things you've discovered in the sales process that you can bring up to overcome any objection. If a customer tells you the price is too high or higher than the competition, before you know what they need and have established your value, where do you go from there?

Selling a suit

I once walked into a high-end clothing store in Austin, TX. That day, the store had on-site a custom-made suit company from New York City. I talked to the guy from the visiting company as I was in the market for a suit. After a few minutes of questions, I asked him how much they cost. He answered, $2,000. I thanked him and told him the suits were nice before walking away. Maybe I did both of us a favor since I didn't intend on spending that much on a suit, but after leaving the store I realized how much differently that conversation could have gone.

Let's say when I ask him about price, he says that it ranges and he can't say for sure until he understands more about my needs. Price varies based on fabric type, color, and type of cut. Also, do I even need a suit? He starts a conversation with me by asking questions and he gets the following answers: What brand of suits do I own now? A few by Hugo Boss. What did I spend on them? $750 each. Do I like them? Actually, after a year the stitching is going bad on two of them and one no longer fits well. What color are they? Two are navy and one is light gray. How often do I wear a suit? Two or three time a month. For what occasions? Mostly business meetings. What do I do for work? I'm a technology salesman. What company? Salesforce.

Based on all of this, he can now offer me a product that has value based on my needs. He can tell me he can provide an America-made suit from the highest quality Italian wool. It will be tailored to my body. His company provides free repairs in the unlikely event the stitching goes bad. The store I am buying it from will also do free alterations forever if my body type changes. The suit can be in dark gray since I don't have that color yet and is a great choice since that color can be worn year-round.

Now when he gets to price, and I tell him $2,000 is over my budget, he has something to fall back on. He can tell me while it is a little more than what I've spent in the past, I've seen the results of buying a cheaper suit. He also knows I work in technology, more specifically with Salesforce, and that I probably make enough to afford it. Don't I want to invest in one great suit I can wear to my sales calls to look better and to give me more confidence? (I had wanted to do exactly that). Whether he gets the sale is still in question, but at least he has something to work with to establish value and fall back on when a price objection comes up. There's a good chance he could have sold me that day. If not, at least he got some practice in for the next customer and gave me a better impression of the company in case I decide in the future to up my budget.

Alternatively, I might have told him that I already own a few suits but rarely wear them and I'm relatively happy with them when I do. I might have said those suits were purchased cheaply. If that's the case then I'm not the right customer. He shouldn't waste his time because he's not going to make the sale. He can tell me it sounds like I don't need a new suit and that he wouldn't even feel comfortable selling me one. As a salesperson, walking away from an opportunity can sometimes be the most fulfilling thing you'll do. As Apple founder Steve Jobs said, it's the 100 things he didn't do that was his true innovation.

Budget vs. Price

Another difference between budget and price is that when discussing the customer's budget at the beginning, it can change as you progress towards the sale. In the example above, my budget started at $750, but after learning about the value of the suit, I am more willing to increase what I'd pay. It doesn't work that way if a salesman starts with their price. It's more difficult to start by telling the customer a cost, and then increase it later in the process. Even if you are offering them more, customers want to fix the price to their budget, whereas a salesman wants to fix the customer's budget to their price. How many times have you gone to buy something, knowing what the price is, only to get annoyed when you learn about all the add-ons you need? Had you known the all-in cost from the beginning, it's easier to plan for that and come down than the other way around. The budget the customer starts with is just a ballpark as to what they can pay but is rarely the price the end up paying. This is true at the most basic level of negotiating the cost of a shirt at an outdoor market, to the price of a car, to the price of a multi-million-dollar technology solution.

The key to note is that at the beginning of the sales process, it's the salesperson asking budgeting questions, for example, how much money have you allocated to this project? Who owns the budget? Is procurement involved in the decision-making process? Will an RFP be required for this project? It's important to ask about budget before you are asked about your price. It's important to beat them to it so you can drive the discussion. It shows a level of maturity to bring it out into the open. It saves you time to find out if they can pay for your service, and if not, how they can find budget.

A pricing question is the prospect asking *you* questions about what your product costs. Simply that question is, "What is your price?" This question is asked by a prospect in just about every first call a salesperson has. It's not a fault of the customer. It's normal for them to want to get this out of the way early so they know if they can afford what you are selling. If I go into an Apple store the first thing I'm going to look at is the cost of a computer before I move forward with additional questions that will lead me to buy it.

The mistake is that salespeople answer this question. If you give a customer a hard number as to what your product costs, even if it's a firm price that can't be negotiated, you are not doing your job very well. If you are asked that question in a first call, it's highly likely you do not know nearly enough about this customer to even know if your product is right for them. I'd rather ask everything I need to know to determine if this customer is a good fit for my product, and if not, end the call before price is ever discussed. If I'm a good salesperson I am not going to jam a product into a customer's business if it's not right for them. This is bad business that will result in long-term headaches for you and your customer service team, and bad word of mouth about you and your product.

If a product is right for a customer, you still don't know what version of your solution to sell them. Chances are you have several ways to modify your product to meet their needs. If I go into a BMW dealership and ask how much a certain model costs, and he replies that it starts at $30,000, the salesman has done both himself and me a disservice. The answer to that question should not be a hard number but should be about what I am looking for. Why that model? What add-ons do I want? Am I open to buying used? What other cars am I considering? The last question is important since it gives the seller a sense of how serious the buyer is. Some might warn that will give the idea to the buyer to look at other products, but it's more than likely that they already are. And no salesperson should be worried if a competitor gets involved if they have a great product.

Create urgency

As you start to know about what a customer wants, a great way to establish value is to create a sense of urgency. Convince the customer that they need to buy now because of all the value your product brings and how much use they will get out of it. Have you ever needed a new piece of clothing, say a jacket, but waited too long into the winter season to purchase it? Every day that goes by where you are cold because you don't have the jacket reduces the value it brings when you do buy it. By creating urgency, it gets people to act earlier. The man selling me the suit could have asked when my next sales call was and urged me to get the suit now so it can be ready in time for that meeting. This is also helpful because salespeople can be fragile to time. The more time that goes by the more things that can come up to prevent the customer from buying. They can be in the form of a competitor, negative information about your product or company, or another pressing need coming up for the client that takes priority over buying your product.

It's okay to create a little fear in the customer as well. It's no different than an advertisement that encourages you to act right away to inspect your air conditioner in Texas before it breaks down in the middle of the summer. Just be strategic about it. In the example I gave last chapter about the university in Missouri, there are plenty of situations I could have mentioned that might be the next crisis they would have to deal with that would require them needing the social media-monitoring tool. But examples aren't even necessary. No one can predict the next crisis that will come, but they can predict how they will be hurt by it, and implement solutions to minimize the damage.

Discounting

I have a long history of discounting. So long it's earned me the nickname of "slasher" and "cutter" from my peers. I often resorted to cutting price because I wasn't always the best at establishing value and differentiating my solution. Instead, I resorted to discounting as the easy and lazy way to close a deal. While this got me a lot of deals,

I do not advise others to follow my lead. Had I gone back to many of those deals, I would have been much more focused on establishing value than cutting price.

Two examples showcase this. The first was in 2010 right after I was hired by McGraw-Hill. I was thrown into a competitive situation where a biology department was deciding what they were going to choose as their new introductory textbook. It was a huge sale covering 1,500 students a year and worth more than $200,000. The incumbent book I was up against was the leading intro biology text on the market.

Both companies were asked to meet with the committee and present their text and any materials that came with it. McGraw-Hill had two intro books and I knew some people on the committee liked one book and some liked the other. I chose to lead with the first book as the one they should consider. I quickly realized the Advocates and Talkers wanted the other one, so I abruptly changed course to pitch that book. That was the right result, but shows how poor of a salesman I was to have no idea going into the meeting what book the vocal people would favor, and only adjusting after I realized it.

As I continued to work the sale, it became obvious the incumbent book was winning. Some people did like my book and others still wished the other book of mine was the one they were considering. I really had no chance to win the sale, until the "slasher" came to town. I showed up to campus two days before the final vote and simply told everyone that I could reduce the price of my book by 20%. That was a big deal, since after the markup from the school bookstore, I was going to save each student over $50. I sold the value of the price reduction as hard as I could. I paid no attention to the content of my book and if it was right for them. I got people excited about finally fighting back against the high price of textbooks by choosing mine.

Although it's ironic that the faculty were so excited to choose a book that was lower in cost, but published by one of the companies responsible for the high cost to begin with.

I ended up winning the sale thanks to coming in last minute with the price break. It's important to note that when doing a price break to do it as close to when the decision is being made as possible, but not too late to where they have already decided. You also don't want to do it too early so there is less of a chance one of your competitors can come in and match the price or continue to sell why their option is better and worth the extra money.

A year later I was in a similar situation. This time it was a chemistry department selecting a book to be used for their intro courses covering 3,000 students a year. At $150 cost per student, this was going to be close to a $500,000 sale. I worked all the committee members, most of whom were unenthusiastic to say the least about switching books based on their reactions to discussing the selection process. They didn't care at all about what I had to offer.

As I worked the process, I knew I wasn't going to win without doing something drastic. I couldn't get anyone to see the value of my book or care enough to adopt the technology that came with it, which was good stuff. I had no Advocates and no compelling reason to get them to make the switch. I had nothing to sway them in my direction, so I went right for the price cut. I went to the head of the department a week before the decision was to be made and told him I could cut the price of the book by 30% to be substantially less than the competition. He decided for the entire department to switch to my book. This shows how the FDM can have more say than all the Talkers, Advocates, and Voters combined.

The list of these situations goes on. Another professor called me towards the end of a semester to tell me they were not going to use the new edition of my book, and were switching to a competitor. This was a shock since I considered it a sure thing and hadn't visited those customers like I would have had I known the situation was competitive. At that point, all I could do was cut the price. I did by 25% and she said she would stay.

While cutting price can get you some sales in the short term, it's not a strategy that is sustainable or one that should be used as a first resort. If you are negotiating and must bend a little, that's a different story, but to go out of your way to reduce the cost makes you look weak and devalues your solution. It tells the customer you know you have an inferior product and all you can do to win the deal is cut the price. Take the suit example. Had the guy told me he could reduce the price from $2,000 to $1,000, to get closer to my budget, it would have sent alarm bells off that something was fishy. Is the suit really that good if he can cut the price like that? Or is it a gimmick he's using to scam me? Or is he just desperate?

Additionally, discounting doesn't always help get sales in the long term. While it might get you in the door and make a customer realize it's a good product, and lead to more sales, often the opposite happens. In the example of the chemistry book, after it was sold I still could not get anyone to use the technology because they never wanted to use the book in the first place. Using the technology is what keeps a book in place since it's much harder for a department to change if they are also using your software. (It's a lot harder to switch from your iPhone when you also have a MacBook and an iPad). As of this writing several years later, that department has switched back to the book they were using before. Additionally, the biology professors from the first example also have since gone back to their old book, showing that the price discount was not a good long-term strategy.

Wow them

If you can, you want to make yourself be the real value. Sell yourself, which is after all, your real job. If you can do something memorable, even if it has nothing to do with your product, your prospect will include it as part of the criteria they use to evaluate your product. This can be done through relationship building. People want to buy from others they like and will do so even if the solution is inferior to the competition. You can also wow them through tangible items. Since I was never the best at driving relationships, I preferred that route.

In one example, I was presenting to a committee of professors who were seeking a new English grammar book to use for their 5,000 freshman students. My presentation was to be held the day after my biggest competitor. Both were held at noon so each company planned to provide lunch catered by the school. My competitor chose to go with cold sandwiches, which was the standard for most presentations. But I decided to go with the most expensive option, which consisted of a deliciously cooked chicken, salad, hot sides, and beverage options of water, tea, and juice. There were even freshly baked cookies. All served on real plates with silverware and cloth napkins. The decision makers were mostly part-time professors who rarely got treated to such a nice meal, and they were ecstatic. It became such a big deal that they asked to hold off on the presentation so we could all sit and eat and talk like we were a family. It was incredible. That experience brought value to their life. There is no question that decision played a bigger factor in me getting the sale than anything about my product.

A similar example had me presenting another English handbook to a committee against two competitors. We were the last to present and my book was called, *The Little Penguin Handbook*. The books were all pretty much the same and there was little to differentiate one versus the other. So I decided to put together little gift baskets that included a DVD of the movie, *March of the Penguins,* along with a little stuffed penguin toy and other goodies. When the faculty saw this they went nuts with excitement. One remarked how much his son was going to love the penguin. I brought value to his child! This was way more effective than just talking about the value of my product. I left the presentation with the room loving me, and shortly after that, I was informed that I won the sale.

Gifts don't always work out, though. In another case, I was selling different products to two separate groups of decision makers that worked in the same department. One was a current customer I was trying to keep and the other was a new customer. During the process, I purchased for the current customer a brand-new DVD player (this was 2005) since they mentioned they needed it for one of their classrooms. They were thrilled, but the other group was very upset. They saw it as a clear violation of ethics and that I was trying to sway them. Others were just jealous they didn't get one for their classroom. The lesson here is knowing the politics involved when offering gifts.

Walk away happy, or not

The quote that opens this chapter is saying that if both parties are happy after making a deal, then it's obvious an equal deal was made. If both parties are not happy, then an equal deal was also made since neither side thinks they got the better end. It's too bad every deal can't be decided by having someone cut the piece of cake in half and the other decides which half they want.

But as a salesperson it's best to strive to give your customer a fair deal, and in turn, get a fair deal for you. It will create positive energy that carries with you in everything you do. Taking short cuts to the lowest price leaves someone on the short end of the deal, or leaves someone feeling happy at the expense of another. It's the Wal-Mart economy where everyone wants the lowest price, but that low price means someone is not getting a fair share. There's a reason that pair of jeans is $10, and it's usually not because that's the fair price for everyone involved in producing and selling those jeans. Someone in the chain is getting the short end. But the cost of buying cheap is always more expensive in the end to everyone, including the buyer who is likely going to have to replace those jeans sooner than if they just invested in a nicer pair from the start. Focus on your value first, and attract those that see it the same way.

Chapter 8:
Don't Email the Proposal

Now that you've got the sale close to the finish line, you need to seal the deal. How to make it official will vary, but this step typically involves delivering a proposal that spells out everything the selling company is providing that leads to a contract or order form. For the purposes of this chapter I'll use the word "proposal" to refer to the last step required to close the deal.

Salespeople obviously love getting to the proposal stage. It means they are at the point where the customer's needs have been defined and the solutions have been agreed upon. All the calls and hard work finally get put into a tangible asset to provide to the customer. Delivering the proposal also means you've negotiated price. You can't help but think of your commission.

But salespeople can make the mistake of not delivering the proposal in the same thoughtful way they went about getting to it. They assume the prospect knows what's in it and send it without reaffirming its contents. This can happen if the prospect is located far away and the most efficient means to get the proposal to them is via email. But emailing the proposal to ask for the sale is a fatal mistake. When I say fatal, it means your deal is being sent off to die with the click of the send button. Deals rarely get confirmed after sending a proposal by email, at least not ones where you weren't certain you were getting it already.

The black hole

Emailing a proposal takes away any leverage a salesperson has over the customer. Prospects are often just as eager to get the proposal as the salesperson is to send it. The prospect might be truly ready to buy, they might want a starting point to further negotiate, or they might need your proposal to compare with a competitor. Whatever the reason, unless you are pushing them to get to the proposal prematurely, the prospect does have genuine interest.

But when you email the proposal it's going into a black hole. You have no idea what the prospect is doing with it. Are they looking at everything in it? Do they understand it? Who are they sharing it with and do those people understand your value? Maybe all they are doing is looking for the price and judging whether it's too expensive, even if it's a fair price and is exactly what they need. You can't trust they will follow-up with you to discuss it further. It's essential to ask for their attention when presenting the proposal, and you must show strength to do it. Tell them you cannot send it unless a call or meeting is set up to walk through it and answer any questions they have.

Sending the proposal through email also sets the precedent for how you will be communicating with your customer as you work to close the deal from there. Once you send it via email, then getting them to commit to calls later is going to be more difficult. I worked a deal with Salesforce where I had emailed the proposal. The customer asked me to and I agreed since I thought the sale was in the bag. We had just spoke a few days before about everything that was going to be in it and she told me they would be moving forward. But even then, I should have set up another call to confirm everything in it and asked her more questions to get it closed. After I sent it, our communication was reduced to me emailing her every few days asking if she was ready to buy. I knew there was a problem because any time a salesperson is emailing a customer asking if they made a decision, it means the customer is not buying from that salesperson. If they were, they would have already reached out. Not surprisingly, I did not get the sale. Looking back on it, I wish I had exhibited strength and told her I would not send the proposal until we set up another call to walk through each part of it with all the decision makers, and explicitly asked for the sale.

Customers have told me via email that I am getting a sale. They will reach out this way to tell you they are ready to buy. It just doesn't happen the other way. Think about if you are selling a large technology deal and you email the customer asking if they decided. The reply will never be, "Oh, thanks for emailing and reminding us we need to make a decision. And yes, by the way, we are going with your company, we just forgot to tell you." When a customer is ready, they will be the one letting you know.

Do it in person

An in-person meeting is the way to get a deal closed. This can sometimes be difficult if the prospect is located far away and you can't travel there. You might have a territory that covers the whole country. The example I just mentioned was with a customer located in Missouri when I was in Texas. But if the size of a deal is large enough and you really can close it, then you must get your face in the place. If an in-person meeting is not possible, then at a minimum, you should be setting up a phone or video call with your customer to walk them through what you've sent and to ask and answer questions. Doing this allows you to ask for the sale. You can look your prospect in the eye, read their body language, and hear their voice for clues. If they are not committing, you can ask what is holding them back. If you are a good player, live poker is always better than the online version since you can read your opponent.

Since the proposal can also be the first time you are presenting a price to the customer, it's even more important to set up a meeting with them to review everything. It's a great opportunity to ensure they remember all the value they are getting with your solution. If they are not ready to commit to buying, you can also ask questions that can close the gap. What is the proposal missing? What do we need to do today to have you commit to us? What number do we need to be at to close this deal? How does our proposal compare to the competition? Asking these kinds of open-ended questions can help you gain information about why they will not pull the trigger.

The face-to-face doesn't even need to be at the end of the process when you are trying to close the sale, but at some point during the process you need to meet your customers. In the end, it is the salesperson they are buying more than the product. Few people will buy from someone they have never met or don't like.

Two lost sales

The first example of a deal I lost after emailing the proposal involved selling to a university in Texas. I had just been hired at this company and one of the first deals I was thrown into was at the proposal stage. I had the prospect rushing me for pricing because she needed to share it with her colleagues and compare it to the other proposals they had. After going back and forth with the customer and my internal team, I was finally able to put everything together. When I informed the prospect it was ready and wanted to walk her team through it, she requested that I email it and then we could set up a call with everyone. This is what I did.

I was then told the proposal looked good and the prospect would let me know when they decided. They no longer felt they needed to talk. For the next six months, I was following up via email and phone, getting short, non-committal answers as to what was going on in their decision process. I was asking myself why I rushed to get them the pricing when they had no timeline on deciding. Worse yet, I was in a silo with that one decision maker and had no idea who the other stakeholders were and what they were thinking.

What a good salesperson would have done would have been to not send the proposal at all. A good salesperson would have never even given pricing without calling a meeting with the Point Person, FDM, and as many of the other decision makers as possible. Rather than be at the beck and call of the customer and do whatever they wanted me to, I would have asked for something in return. This could have been done very simply and directly in a call like this:

Me: Prospect, I really appreciate the opportunity to get you this proposal. When it's ready tomorrow, let's set up a call with the team that is making the decision with you.

Prospect: Can you just send it to me to share with everyone? Since I'm the main point of contact, I'll relay the information to them.

Me: Prospect, I appreciate that but I do want to be sure that everyone understands the proposal and gets a chance to ask me their questions. My manager will not even let me send the proposal without setting up a call with the committee and us.

Prospect: And I understand your need. But I will not be able to do that. I'd just prefer if you can send it to me to pass to the team and we will let you know what questions we have. I can assure you the committee will understand your solution and will be able to ask questions when needed.

Me: I do trust you will ensure this, Prospect, but I just can't send it without setting up a call or meeting. I'll be in the area tomorrow so can we set up a meeting? Or let me know when is a good time for a quick call.

You can use whatever cadence you deem appropriate but the point is the same that as a salesperson, you deserve something in this exchange too. I'd rather never send the proposal than send it only to be in limbo for the next six months, and then get told they chose a competitor. That's exactly what happened. Of course, the result of this was just a symptom of the fact that I had no relationship to begin with to ask for the meeting. But if you have no relationship with the client and don't think you will get the sale, then it's more reason to take a risk and tell them you will not send the proposal until the meeting is set up.

Another example of trying to close without the meeting comes from a time I was selling to a prospect in Louisiana. My contact loved the company I was with and was sold on the product based on research she had done. We built a great relationship. As the process went on, other decision makers got involved who I didn't know as well, and who were leaning towards another company. I set up a couple of phone calls with them but was unable to gain the type of momentum I had with my initial contact. As the process went on, the customers chose the competitor.

Now there were several factors that led to me losing, some out of my control and some that were my own mistakes. But the only thing I regret was not going to visit them. Those calls I had with the other decision makers needed to be in person. It was my only way to build a relationship and get them to believe in me. If I had no differentiator with my product, then the differentiator could have been me. I should have gone there when I first heard about them being involved. The meeting might have happened in the middle of the process, and not at the end, but I may not have needed to go back. But by the time I did offer to visit with them it was too late as I had lost the momentum I had, and the deal was heading towards the competitor.

No proposal at all

In the next chapter, I'll again reference when I was selling my condo in Austin. When I was searching for a realtor, I called two people and met with each on back to back days.

The encounters could not have been more different. The first was with one of the flashier companies in Austin that boasts about being the biggest and best and guaranteeing your home gets sold. They advertise themselves alongside Barbara Corcoran, the well-known real estate mogul from the show *Shark Tank*. They sent a young and aggressive guy to meet with me who told me everything I wanted to hear, some of which was not accurate, before he pulled out the contract for me to commit. I told him I was not ready. The other realtor was an older lady; a soft spoken, yet stern Texan, who works independently. She was honest, trustworthy, and best of all, didn't even bring a contract for me to sign. Her style was one of really connecting to her customers and getting them to want to work with her. It worked because after that meeting I told myself there was no one else I wanted selling my place.

A problem with the proposal is that working to get to one makes you less creative in how you can get the sale. Like trying to get to the demo, by fixating yourself on getting to the proposal, you've already determined where the sales process is going. By allowing the process to run a more natural course, you can be more fluid and adapt to the situation as it changes. Unless the prospect asks for a proposal, then it should not be something that the salesperson is working to get to.

I've seen a lot of deals get closed that never even had a proposal. If it's a product, then it's even less likely you need one since the prospect can see and touch what you are selling and will decide based on those merits. If you are selling a technology or service, then you might need one to quantify everything it includes. But if you've worked the process correctly and earned your customer's trust, established value, and have access to all the decision makers, it rarely requires all that to be put into a formal proposal. They'll just ask for the contract. The work you've done speaks for itself and the prospect will have a firm understanding of your solution without needing it on paper. This is especially true if you connect them to other satisfied customers. Anyone that does need it on paper that you haven't talked to is likely someone who has a say in the decision, and your lack of access to them is a sign that you will not get the deal.

Not getting a sale because you emailed the proposal is a symptom of a larger problem. Maybe you haven't established enough value, you don't know their real needs, you are way off on budget, or you don't have strong relationships. You might never get those things for whatever reasons. But when you have a chance to have the customer's full attention, you need to meet in person to gather as much information as possible about how you can close the deal.

Let it flow

When I did close a deal the process moved naturally. It's like water in a river that comes up against a rock and simply flows around it. There is no forcing the process. When I worked to schedule the initial discovery call, it didn't take countless attempts to secure a time with the prospect. They were the ones setting the time and didn't cancel because it was a priority for them. When it came to finding out more about their needs, the prospect was open to answering all my questions. When I asked about budget, they told me what they could spend. Getting this information didn't require manipulation or doing things that were contrary to what will naturally occur. One call led to the next and the next and before I knew it, the customer was ready to buy.

A deal I closed at Arkansas State University exemplifies this. Their online education division needed a solution to record all their technology support tickets. They had a need, I had a solution, and it all came together without any force. It took work and persistence but it all happened so easily. When I asked to include others on our call, the main contact got them there. When they asked about pricing, they had no problem paying what we asked and they told me in very clear terms how the budget would be procured. Every step of the process flowed naturally to the last step. It was so easy to communicate with them that when I asked my contact if they could sign by a specific date so I could close the sale by the end of the month, she had no problem going to her boss to make sure it happened.

There's a popular quote about life being 90% preparation and 10% execution. The thinking is that if you prepare thoroughly and get everything you need set up, the action it takes to get what you need done happens so fast. Think about cooking dinner. Most of the time is prepping all your ingredients and tools, and the actual cooking process can happen in minutes. It's the same with a sale. If you properly do what I've described in the preceding chapters, then actually closing the deal can happen quickly. It might take days, weeks, months or years to work the sale, but just minutes for a customer to sign on the dotted line.

Chapter 9:
A Sale is Never Complete

When the work is done he does not dwell with it.

-Lao Tzu, Tao Te Ching

You've closed the deal. Congratulations! It's an amazing feeling to be told you won. You feel great about yourself and you get to celebrate with your new customer, your co-workers, and your friends and family. You've also bought yourself more time in the job. Most importantly, you know a big commission check is on the way. It's the best situation for a salesperson to be in. But don't celebrate too much as many salespeople do. There is still a lot to do beyond the time the customer signs the contract. The work is never really finished.

A mistake salespeople can make after closing a deal is to stop working it as hard as they did to close it. They dwell on their success, which is dangerous because it can lead to one resting on their laurels and getting complacent. Instead, when a sale is closed, they need to immediately start thinking about what else needs to be done. A good salesperson knows the process is just starting when a deal is closed and there are a multitude of reasons why working the sale beyond the close is so important.

Resellers

Some industries involve resellers. Resellers buy your product in bulk from your company at a discount and then resell it on the open market. In these cases, you need to work with your customer to ensure they buy your product from your company and not them. In 2007, I sold an English book to the University of Notre Dame for a class of 500 students totaling $30,000. I was so excited I drove two hours to their campus and personally delivered 100 copies of the book to distribute to the faculty and teaching assistants. I did this with a herniated disc and remember walking across campus in terrible pain in the middle of January in Northern Indiana to show my appreciation.

What happened later was a punch to the gut. Since the book had just been published, I assumed that the University bookstore would have to purchase it from our company for classes in the fall semester. I did nothing to ensure this and just waited all summer for the order to come in. I hadn't seen the order placed by mid-July so I called the store and asked when they were placing the order. They told me they secured all the copies from a reseller and needed only 20 copies from me. It was devastating. All that work for nothing, and all I needed to do was work with my customer to ensure that the bookstore ordered the book from my company. This could have been very easy had I just told the customer I couldn't furnish the free copies to the staff unless the order was placed through my company. I could have delivered half the books and then sent the other half once the order went through. But instead I got too confident and didn't do the most basic thing necessary to get the revenue.

Competition like this lurks in every industry. When you're ready to buy something it's common to check a dozen websites and retailers to see who offers the lowest price. This happens on a micro scale when searching for a vacuum cleaner to much larger purchases of a car. Whatever you are selling, it's important to get your customer to buy from you. You can do this through quantitative incentives like a rebate or free add-ons, or through qualitative incentives like great customer service. Regarding the latter, people will buy from you even at a higher price if they trust they can come to you if something goes wrong with the product. This is why people love shopping at REI for camping gear. They tend to be more expensive but their staff is so helpful and knowledgeable and they have a one-year return policy. I know that's why I go there over the competition.

Upselling

Other businesses bring the opportunity to upsell with companion products. Upselling is perhaps the best opportunity to add more revenue after the initial sale. First off, you have your customer in the mood to buy. Once someone makes one purchase they are more likely to make a second. If a customer spends $200 on a pair of jeans, now is the time to get them to drop $50 for a new belt. Once people open their wallet to make a purchase, they lose their inhibition to buy. There's also less incremental cost to add on another product. If you're spending $30,000 on a new car, what's another $2,000 to add the navigation? Especially when it takes the monthly payment from $500 to only $530.

Upselling is also important because your customer might think they need to buy another product to go with their original purchase. My mother managed a Swarovski crystal store for many years and was one of the company's top performers because she never let a chance slip by to get the customer to buy more. If they bought a necklace, then she would sell them a bracelet and earrings to go with it. The customer felt like they wanted the complete package to look their best.

Future projects

Another important reason to keep working with your customer beyond the sale is so they will give you future projects. An example of this comes from my own experience as a customer. I purchased my first home in 2012, a condo in downtown Austin. I worked closely with a realtor that was referred to me by a close friend. I liked the realtor and she found me a dream home. But when I decided to sell five years later, I didn't hire her again. The reason was that she never checked in with me after the sale to see how I was doing and build a relationship. She did some minor things like send me a small gift after the original purchase and included me on her monthly mailings. But I never felt close enough to her to where there was no one I'd rather work with. It would have been simple for her to keep my business had she written me a personal email from time to time and built a true relationship. If she had, I would have felt compelled to work with her. Instead, I just viewed her as a commodity and that there were many other realtors I could work with. And to her, I just became another sale. It cost her the chance for a nice commission check.

The textbooks I sold to universities would publish into new editions every 2-3 years. In Chapter 7, I referenced a sale I won for an English grammar text when I was able to "wow" my decision makers with the amazing lunch. In that example, they were using the incumbent book for several years and everyone was very happy with it. There was no reason to change. Plus, switching grammar texts takes a lot of work and time for professors. I was brand new to the territory and should have never been able to get the sale had the incumbent salesperson, who was in the territory for 10 years, kept selling his book between editions.

I started calling on those professors in December, as they were planning to decide a few months later. During that month the incumbent rep, realizing he now had competition, went around to all the committee members with holiday cards with a personal note in each one thanking them for using his book for so many years. The problem was that many of those professors had not seen that rep since he sold the previous edition of the book three years prior. Now that the new edition of his book was publishing and it was a competitive situation, he decided to finally go to everyone and show his face. It turned a lot of people off who thought he was insincere and didn't trust him. He didn't count on a young salesperson from a rival company moving in on his business. It really hurt him that he didn't have a relationship with his customer beyond the original sale he made, and I exploited that big time.

New "editions" happen in other industries, for example, auto and electronics, who release updated models every year. Clothing is another example where a designer produces a new line for the upcoming summer season. To keep their customer's attention, these companies need to continue advertising and building a brand between editions so their customers only come to them when they need a new car, computer, or pair of jeans.

Referrals

You're going to need current customers to refer new business to you. They will not do this until well after they've bought your product and know it's good and can trust you. You earn trust by staying in contact after you've gotten them to buy. When you do this, you get referrals. It just comes naturally where you can either ask for an introduction or the customer does it on their own. It's not forced and doesn't look like you just want the sale to ask for a referral. The best salespeople go a mile deep and an inch wide with their existing base and more business flows from that. The best way you can do this it to take care of those that have already bought from you. I know this because I would go a mile wide and an inch deep, and seldom got the referrals I could have, and have seen others get.

Implementation

In Chapter 1, I referenced the sale I made with G&K Services and how once I made the sale I stopped working. I didn't pay any attention to the implementation of the project. I thought my job was done once the sale was made and it was the responsibility of others to take it from there. This is what a lot of salespeople do. It's not entirely their fault since the structure can call for that. There might be an account manager who services the customer or a service team that implements the product and solves technical problems. Some companies have partners that do the implementation once it's sold. But none of these situations gives the sales rep the pass to not stay in touch with their customer beyond the sale.

Working with your customer during implementation is a great time to accomplish many things. You show you care even though you already sold them. Few things mean more to a customer than to have the salesman reach out just to ask how things are going and if they are happy with how the solution is being set up. It also helps to build the relationship and to build trust.

I know this because I rarely did it, which is why I never had as many add-on sales and referrals as I could have. After you close the deal is the time to go deeper with the customer. Don't just sell and leave them to their own devices. Even if there's a separate team in your company to help with implementation, it's still worth the time to stay in close contact with the customer as they start using your product. This helps not only for the relationship, but also to deepen your understanding of your product and how they are using it.

If I applied this to the things I sold, I see how much that could have helped. Like the example with G&K, I could have met my contractors at every job site to help them install the coating. When I was selling textbooks, I could have called a meeting with my customers two months into them using the book to see how it was going. I wish I had called that kind of meeting to service them as quickly as I called the meeting to sell them. I once had a customer who was using my technology to support processing new customers into their system. But after it was sold I never went in to sell the marketing tools I had to get more customers into their funnel. I blew a perfect opportunity to learn about their business and show I was invested in their success to eventually sell a companion product that could have enhanced their operations.

Selling with no deal on the table can also be helpful because it gives you a true, bottom up approach to making a sale. It allows you to learn about your customer without the pressure of making a sale. If you don't know enough about the business you are in, it provides a great learning opportunity. Get to know them. Ask how their job is. Take them out for a drink or meal. Ask to track one of the employees to see what their day-to-day life is like. When I sold call center services for Blackboard, one of the first things I asked to do was go to the centers and sit in on calls for several hours to understand the job of the person taking the calls. This helped me relate to my eventual prospect to share stories of how our solution really works rather than just repeat whatever I was told. The time to sell is just as much when there is no current opportunity, because the truth is that there is always another opportunity.

One of the worst things you can do, not just in sales, but generally in life, is to get complacent. Once you get comfortable you get lazy, and once you get lazy you start to lose what you've achieved. And now that you are lazy, it's hard to get it back. To prevent this, one must always be aware of where they want to go and not where they have been. Once you know this, you need to know what it takes to get there. It involves a plan and a strategy, and it also involves being open to change.

Chapter 10: Plan to Change Jobs

I'm a great quitter. It's one of the few things I do well.
I come from a long line of quitters.
My father was a quitter. My grandfather was a quitter.
I was raised to give up.

-George Costanza

It's good to have an exit strategy in your sales job because it's unlikely you will be in the same position or company for more than a few years. Sales is transitory. It's the nature of the salesperson who is dynamic and likes a new challenge. It's also the nature of the job as companies will promote you, competitors will hire you, or you might get fired or decide to quit to pursue something else. According to a 2015 study by the job search company Glassdoor, where 1,000 salespeople were surveyed, 55% spent no more than four years at any one company and 68% said they'd be looking for a new job in the next year. Just don't make it a self-fulfilling prophecy and leave before you have to. A lot of the movement also comes from lack of patience. Since it can take a full year to be fully productive as a sales rep, this length of time can cause a rep to get frustrated, give up, and leave. Companies often similarly lose patience and part ways prematurely.

My father was not a quitter and neither was my grandfather. But I did job-hop a lot during my career. I made nine moves to new positions in 15 years. Each one had its own unique situation. I left Thermal-Chem for Pearson since the latter was a much larger company offering better compensation. I left McGraw-Hill for Wiley, also for more money, and for a better title. I left Wiley for

Colloquy because my position was moved to New York and I didn't want to leave Austin. I'm content with every move I made and do not regret any of my decisions except for how I left Blackboard. I regretted the decision because I didn't go out on my terms and chose money over my integrity in how I left.

Reasons to take a new job

If you're good at sales, other companies will recruit you to bring your talents to their organization, even if you are not looking for a new job. The industry you choose will be like a sports league where players frequently move between teams who provide higher pay and all kinds of great incentives. For the salesperson, there are three main reasons why you would take another job: better pay, better location, and a better title. The last reason may be the least important to you if, like me, you couldn't care less what you're called so long as you made great money and love where you live. But for some, being a "Sales Representative" or "Account Executive" wasn't enough, and they needed a position like "Solutions Engineer," "Senior Consultant," or "Product Specialist."

Regarding pay, this is subjective and entirely on you to decide what will make you happy. My suggestion is to look at the positive asymmetry with the new job and think of it as a graph. If the x-axis is input (time and amount of work) and the y-axis is overall happiness (mainly composed of money and perks), what does the line look like and how does it compare to your current job? The latter might be a straight line. If you put in the same amount of work you'll safely get a consistent return over the same period. Now what does the line look like for the new position? Will it initially take more work but then the pay off will be much higher? If so, maybe the upside in the new job is worth it. But, since the new job is a big unknown, it could also crash and burn.

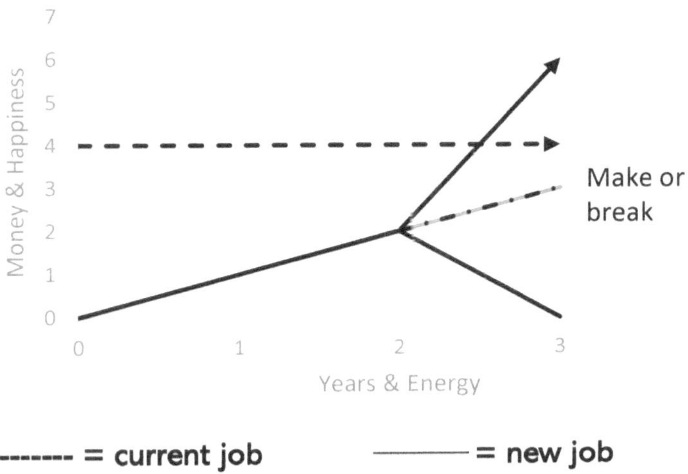

------- = current job   ——————— = new job

But you also want to consider other factors that make up overall happiness like the culture of the new company, the onboarding process, where you'd live or how happy you are with your current manager. You might be able to make a lot more money in the new job, but if you think your new boss will be the Jerk, then perhaps the extra pay is not worth it. Maybe you'll grow unhappy if you stay in your current job because it's not exciting anymore. These qualitative aspects can only be determined by you and are sometimes harder to judge than quantitative stuff like money.

I had to face this decision in 2006 when another publisher tried to lure me away from Pearson. I was living in Ohio and the new company had a job in Chicago, where I wanted to move back to. The new manager did a great job building a relationship with me by sending me gifts from Chicago after I agreed to take the position. When I told Pearson I was leaving, they came back with an offer for a job in Chicago. I had to compare both jobs, with the new company offering a little more money and I knew how excited they were for me to join. It would have been a fun challenge. But in the end, the comfort I had with Pearson and not wanting to risk the unknown of the new company made me decide to stay. Plus, as I mentioned in Chapter 2, I felt the upside with the territory in Chicago was worth sticking around for.

Performance Improvement Plan

Sometimes it's the company that wants you to leave. When this happens, you will likely receive a Performance Improvement Plan (PIP) rather than be outright fired, unless you did something egregious that warrants it. A PIP documents the reasons your performance is falling short and what you need to do to improve. It typically has specific examples of this. I received a PIP at two different companies and gave PIPs to two of my reps when I was a manager at Pearson. Here's an example of one page from a real PIP I received:

To: Rashad Daoudi, Sales Executive NAHE Services Sales
From: ███████████, VP Student Lifecycle Services
cc: ███████████, VP Education Services, ████████, HR Business Partner Director
Date: ████████
Subject: Performance Improvement Plan

Rashad, the purpose of this memo is to notify you that your performance is not meeting the expectations of your role in several significant areas. As you know, we have had conversations over the last several weeks about your role and your performance. We have talked about the ways in which your performance is not meeting expectations. I have not seen the improvement and progress that I would expect.

Overall, the concerns fall into the following 3 major areas:

1. **Proactive Client Opportunity Assessment & Planning**:
As an Education Services Sales Executive, our expectations are that you have the ability to identify, scope, and strategize detailed capture strategies for opportunities within your assigned accounts and region. You are not meeting these expectations, as demonstrated by your inaccurate assessment of your Q2 pipeline and your insufficient preparation for customer meetings.

- For example, in reviewing your pipeline with ████████ during the week of 5/4, we identified that the quality and depth of your Q2 sales opportunity pipeline needed more attention. We expressed concern about your assessment of the stage and maturity of opportunities in your pipeline. In particular, you estimated that the Central New Mexico CC opportunity had a 50% probability of closing in Q2 while the client had not identified budget. We responded that this opportunity was not at the appropriate stage and that we believed your diagnosis was inaccurate.
- In preparation for the onsite meeting with ████████████████ on 5/27, you emailed me on 5/25 with initial thoughts on the presentation and indicated that you would put together some slides. After not seeing anything from you, I took the lead on preparing the presentation and informed you prior to and after the meeting that I was disappointed in your planning and preparation for this important meeting.

Moving forward, I must see substantial growth and improvement in your assessment and planning.

- Over the next 30 days, I expect that you will provide demonstrable examples in which you proactively drive opportunity planning and capture strategies through a more consistent process. Specifically, I would like you to schedule a 1:1 meeting with me each week to review active client opportunities in your pipeline. During the meeting, you will provide a documented activity plan that includes the following information:
    - o Opportunity name and sales stage assessment (e.g. Suspect   Qualification, Power Sponsor)
    - o Your recommended activities to advance the opportunity to the next stage
    - o Actions that you will take independently and dependencies that you will resolve with support from the client, internal capture team, and/or management to advance the opportunities
    - o Measurable progress milestones and weekly deadlines for each advancement activity
- During this period, if you have any client meetings, you will prepare a document outlining key planning activities and owners to ensure the internal capture team and client are

If you get a PIP, rule number one is not to panic. You probably knew it was coming or you really are that bad and deserve to get fired. If it truly is a shock, then something nefarious might be happening and a manager is trying to get rid of you for unjustified reasons. Or they think some actions you took were wrong that you didn't and they want to replace you with someone else they'd prefer. Whatever the reason, the key is do not get angry. Do not show emotion. It will only hurt your cause and make you look like you are in the wrong. Be professional and tell them you understand and that you'd like to know what steps will be taken next. If you get something like what is pictured above, respond promptly to each point and defend yourself with documentation if possible.

The next step will be a call with your manager who will explain why you are getting the PIP. If you can, record this call. There is a good chance your manager will say something illegal or wrong that will give you some justification to save your job or prolong the process to buy you more time to look for another job. It could also lead to your having grounds to sue. Since a PIP typically includes a list of the reasons why you are receiving it, along with a 30-day plan of action you need to take, a great question to ask is whether completing the PIP will save your job. If a manager says probably not, this is a perfect reply you can use against them. This means the manager has already made up their mind to fire you, which is basically saying the PIP is just a formality. But to the human resources department this is bad since they don't want to look like the company is acting unfairly.

Your next step is to call H.R. to ask them what your options are and to plead your case. Just be aware that H.R. is not your friend in this scenario. They may say they are impartial and act that way, but they are on the side of your manager. In fact, it was them who instructed your manager to put you on a PIP since outright firing can lead to a lawsuit. They ideally want you not to complete it so they can fire you or better yet, have you quit since most companies don't want to pay unemployment. Any negotiation should be done through H.R. only. You might be able to ask for additional pay, if you agree to leave, on top of what you would already get. Consider having a personal lawyer speak with them.

If you do decide to go through with the plan to save your job, understand that your manager will do everything in their power to make you miserable so you do quit. That's what I did at Pearson with one of the reps I put on a PIP. He wasn't planning to leave on his own so during the week following the PIP, I was in his office every hour scrutinizing his every move. I was constantly asking him for reports and updates and calling meetings. This was a huge shift from his previous days of never being bothered by anyone. He couldn't take the micro-managing for very long before he turned in his resignation. If your manager is smart, they will make your life unbearable to where your best option is to leave.

This also happened to me at EyeWonder. I lasted three days before I realized there was no way I was going to meet every day with a manager I disliked so much. So, I just quit. At Blackboard, I tried to do the same, but only this time they replied by telling me they wanted to fire me rather than have me quit. I chose to let them do it since being fired meant I could collect unemployment.

I learned later why this decision was one I regret so much. Deciding to quit was not easy. When I got the PIP, I had planned to fight for my job and also wanted to buy myself more time to find a new job. But after further consideration I chose to quit because I knew the stress that trying to complete the PIP would cause myself and my manager. I thought it was the most honest thing to do and I wanted to go out on my terms. Then as soon as a few thousand dollars was dangled in front of me with the extra money I would get from being fired, I changed my mind. I made the decision to quit to keep my integrity, and a few months after agreeing to be fired, not only was the extra money gone, but so was my integrity.

It was also not so financially advantageous to get fired since when trying to get a future job, telling the new employer I was fired weakens my credibility. I look much stronger if I can tell them I quit because I wanted to go in another direction.

Interviewing

Interviewing is the biggest sale you'll make in the job you are going for. You are selling yourself in the same way you are selling a product, but it requires more creativity than luck to close the deal. How did I get a job that required five years of experience selling Software as a Service (SaaS) when I had only two? How did I increase my salary by $30,000 with one move to another job with the same title? How did I survive every corporate restructuring I've been a part of when so many of my more qualified counterparts were let go?

The answer is phenomenal interviewing skills. In the case of the SaaS job, I read the entire book of the company's

CEO and quoted it at every stage of the process. This included his section about hiring and preferring someone who is ambitious and easier to train than someone with 10+ years of industry experience. I didn't have the required experience so I found another way to get it. Whenever I interviewed I always differentiated myself in a big way by doing something like that. Other times I did keep a job through luck. At Blackboard, I had been with them for four months before a corporate restructuring reduced the number of people on my team from 12 to 8. I was the most recent hire of the 12 but stayed on because the company felt worse if they laid me off since they just hired me. The luck of being the "new guy" kept me in a job.

Interviewing is also about getting ahead of where the interviewers are in the hiring process. Just like a sales process where it's the salesperson's job to paint the vision for the customer, you need to do that for the hiring company. I've made a 90-day plan for every job I've wanted that shows the company exactly what I am going to do to get started. They love that stuff. Would you hire someone with an extensive background or someone with less experience but a bright future that is putting on paper the step-by-step plan they will take to ensure success? I know I'd go with the person with more motivation and put less emphasis on the perfect resume.

It's worth noting that the way in which I got the SaaS job had to do in part to luck and timing. I applied to the job and a few days later got a call back. I was surprised because it was rare for them to grant an interview to people who did not apply through a referral from within the company. But they were interested since I had a lot of experience in higher education, which was the industry they were hiring for. And I had used their product in my previous jobs. The initial call went well which led to another call with the hiring manager. After a few more calls, I found myself as a finalist where I had to make a mock presentation before they offered it to me.

I later found out how lucky my timing had been. A week into starting, whose name do I see as the previous rep I replaced? It was the woman who recruited me to EyeWonder seven years before. She bounced around jobs as much as I had and lasted six months in my current job. It hit me that my manager hired her and it was a disaster. She left right at the time I was looking for a job and I swooped in to take it. I was probably his only candidate in Austin with industry experience. Combine that with my ability to walk and chew gum at the same time and I was hired. Now I had a six-figure salary with one of the largest technology companies in the world. Six months before I was a washed up, recently-fired salesman with little hope for a good-paying job. Luck and circumstance played a major role in that, but I still had to capitalize on the opportunity.

Fake your resume (if needed)

Hopefully you have a strong track record as you apply for other positions. If so, you'll have a great resume which will speak for you. Even if you are not looking for a job, companies will find you especially if you have a LinkedIn account. Recruiters are always looking for talent and will send you messages about new opportunities.

If you don't have the best history, you obviously may not have other companies interested in you. This is where "modifying" your resume is something you need to learn to do. Here are some examples of what I really did at my jobs followed by how I can alter them in a more positive light for my resume:

At EyeWonder:

Put together chairs for the new downtown office

Managed office to ensure positive work environment and efficient use of employee time

At Salesforce:

Attained 28% of FY '17 quota

Sold $180,000 in FY '17

At Colloquy:

Almost closed a deal with the University of Arizona

Closed deal worth $2 million with the University of Arizona

You have the option to fake your sales numbers but the new company could find out as you are asked to talk about your past sales. If you go this route, just make sure to not overdo it. Making your numbers look just good enough without bringing too much attention is the right mixture. Have a story ready to tell to cover yourself.

I did this on my resume under my time at Colloquy when I put that I closed a $2 million deal that never happened. I didn't have any sales when I was there and had to make up something. I did that with a sale big enough to make me credible but didn't draw a ton of questions. Another good strategy is to highlight where you did have success and worry about filling in the gaps if the new company asks. For example, at Blackboard I hit my goal in my first two quarters but not in my last two. When asked about it I was just honest and explained I hit a rough patch. This is a good way to gauge what kind of manager you will have.

If they give you a hard time about it then you probably don't want to work for them anyway.

Another key to the resume is to mix in a lot of bullet points about the peripheral things you did alongside your sales numbers. Examples such as how many cold calls you made a day, how many presentations you did a week, and other qualitative achievements. One of the most attractive highlights I had for new companies was that I had used Salesforce for several years, which was the tool those companies used to manage their sales leads. Companies love hiring someone they don't have to train on their systems.

References

In the next chapter I will talk about relationships and the reality that most of them are designed for nothing more than to help you get a sale. Another important reason to have these relationships is because you are eventually going to need a reference if you are trying to leave your current job. It will be hard to use your manager or others in your current company since you don't want them to know you are leaving. You also may not be able to use anyone at a past job where you left under bad terms. This is where a customer, colleague, or manager you can trust from your current or past jobs will help. Try not to burn bridges whenever you can. Or better yet use someone that you became friends with.

Whether you are exiting your sales job on your terms or not, leaving is a reality that can't be avoided. The question is if you are going to take control of the process or will it take control of you. It's always good to get in front of things. Keep your options open and never turn down a chance to learn about another opportunity. It's like dating. You might be in a happy relationship, but why not take down someone else's number? You may not be looking now, but you might be in six months. And since that is about how long it can take to secure a job, it helps to start that process as early as you can.

Chapter 11: Relationships

Anyone thinking of his own interests and seeking out friendship with this in view is making a great mistake…the thing you described is not a friendship but a business deal.

-Seneca

Along the way of working your sales, it helps to have a network of support to advance and close them. In the best-selling sales book, *Never Eat Alone,* author Keith Ferrazzi says, "What distinguishes highly successful people from everyone else is the way they use the power of relationships—so that everyone wins." The book emphasizes that salespeople can't be as successful as possible if they work on their own. By utilizing co-workers, colleagues, and customers, a salesperson can cultivate meaningful relationships that lead to greater success. Ferrazzi's book is the blueprint for building and leveraging relationships. I don't think there's one thing he doesn't cover about how to use a network to your advantage.

Ferrazzi is right. I know that because my inability to form advantageous relationships within the sales community was a big reason why I was not as successful as I could have been. I couldn't do it because I felt these relationships were centered around closing a sale and rarely felt that any of them were genuine. Because of that I started to not want any part of them. To my customers, I only cared about them as much as I needed to in order to make a sale. For my manager, how much he liked me was as much as my sales numbers were good. To the partner companies I worked with, we only cared about each other as much as we could help the other make a sale. To my colleagues, it was about perpetuating the system we were in that I no longer felt comfortable in.

Be warned that this could happen to you as well. You might find it hard to truly care about others beyond anything other than closing the deal. It might not sit well with you that your worth is based purely on how much revenue you can produce. This dislike will be especially apparent if you are working for companies that are not doing collective good for society.

The more this happens the more this can also seep into your personal life. Your relationships with real friends and family might start to resemble those from your sales world. When you're selling all the time to customers, you are selling to everyone else. It was difficult to spend the whole day showing no weakness, crafting my messages just right, providing solutions to everyone's problems, and then be an authentic person to the ones I love. I couldn't separate the two and you may not be able to either.

I'm not sure how to get around this. I think it helps to have a real belief in yourself and come into sales from a place of love and with a desire to help others. I think staying within a field where you can become an expert is key so you have real expertise to be good at what you do and feel valuable to others. It also helps to be in a field where you feel what you are doing is benefiting all parties involved and doing good for the world.

I'm not going to go into much more detail about this aspect of the relationships you'll encounter in sales. The topic is for another book I'll write someday. Instead, I will focus on a few key ways of how to form and not form the types of relationships you need to help make a sale. Regardless of whether you believe these relationships are real or not, you need to employ various tactics to form them to help you make the sale.

How not to do it

To build these business relationships, there are plenty of tactics I've seen be successful but not always utilized. For one, don't be shortsighted. I learned this mid-way through my career when I was selling advertising. One of the other sales reps asked if I wanted to go out one night with several people who worked with one of the media agencies he called on. I turned him down, and rationalized to myself that if they weren't my clients I didn't need to go out with them.

This was bad thinking for a few reasons. On a personal level, I missed out on a fun night in Chicago. But professionally it was worse since although they were not my customers, I could have met others who were or had those people make introductions for me since everyone knows each other in advertising. I could have also learned about their jobs to take that insight to my customers. Additionally, sales territories work in mysterious ways and there was a possibility I would be calling on that agency in the future. Six months after that night, the sales rep left the company and the media agency was reassigned to me. I had no relationships and was starting from scratch to try to get meetings, rather than having a friendship with them.

Never underestimate building relationships with those who may not be directly involved with your getting a sale. This goes for events you attend where you end up chatting with people who are not at one of your accounts but know someone who is. Like advertising, most industries are close knit and people can make introductions for you. There's also a chance they worked previously at one of your accounts making it more likely they can introduce you or at least give you insight about the account.

Secretaries are another example of overlooking someone important. A lot of times salespeople view them as a way to get to the person they want not realizing the secretary is who they want. Secretaries are a great source of information and if they like you they will be more likely to get you to the decision makers. One time I closed a sale entirely through a secretary who spoke on my behalf to the head of the division, who agreed to purchase my product. She was the closest person to the final decision maker, and by making friends with her, it was as good as calling on the actual person.

Wine and dine 'em

Another example of how I blew a chance to secure a sale through relationship-building also came from my time in advertising. I called on the media agency for Office Max and was invited to meet the media buyer who was preparing a new campaign of online ads for the upcoming holiday season. We had a great meeting and after presenting my solution, he emailed to tell me I was getting the deal. I was so excited I made the grave mistake I talk about in Chapter 9 of assuming the deal was done.

A week later, when I called the agency to tell them I had the contract ready to sign, he informed me that their current vendor came back with a lower price in a bid to keep the business. He said he preferred to stay with them since it was easier than switching to another vendor. I realized what really happened was he used me to threaten that vendor that he was leaving so they would lower their price. He totally played me and I didn't see it coming.

If I had, the result might have been the same, but I could have tried to keep the sale by building a relationship with him. Right after being told they were buying my solution I should have taken him out. As soon as he gave me the good news I could have said let's celebrate at one of the best steak houses in Chicago or at a Cubs game. If he turns me down then I know something is up. People usually don't turn down something like that and if he did go, then it makes it hard for him to turn to me a few days later and give me the bad news, especially if we got drunk together. Bonds can really be formed when you are helping someone throw up directly into the toilet. By not doing something to build the relationship, it did not personalize the process and made it too easy for him to tell me I was not getting the sale.

It's obvious that taking your customers out helps build a relationship. I know because I rarely had personal relationships with my customers because I rarely took them out. Anything that gets you outside of the office is beneficial because it breaks the boundaries of the work relationship and lets both sides put their guards down and really talk (especially if alcohol is involved). I equate this to romancing someone by taking him or her to several places on a first date. Doing this makes the relationship seem like it's been around longer and is stronger because you've been through more together, thus increasing your chances of closing the deal.

Be yourself

Looking back, I wish I had just been myself more. Rather than hide behind the sales wall I created, I could have been more honest. I could have told some customers of the difficulty I had with relationship-building when a sale is involved. They might have respected that and it could have been a point of conversation. By bringing something like that up instead of hiding from it or faking it, it might have relieved some of the pressure I felt.

I also wish I had been more forthcoming that I got a commission on what they were buying. By hiding this I was not being truthful and my customers had a right to know about my motives. Just because money is involved doesn't mean I am lying about what I'm selling but it allows them to more honestly evaluate what I was saying. Plus, it could have been a good sales tactic so they view me as being more honest for disclosing this info. I recall the story of the Texas Attorney General Ken Paxton and the charges of fraud levied against him for not disclosing that he was receiving shares in a company for which he was trying to solicit funds from investors. I remember thinking how corrupt he was before realizing I was no different!

Show you care

If you do care, then show it. If you don't, then try to fake that you do. You have to be completely bought into what you, your company, and the customer are doing. Don't show any sign that you are not 100% on board with what is happening. When you show the utmost confidence, customers will believe it. Reinforce all the slogans. People respond to and respect a person who is sure of what they are saying more than what they are actually saying. This also makes for keeping your job as companies love employees who tow the company line.

You can also be a wealth of information to your customer. Send them articles you read or share stories about what another customer is doing. Create a Twitter account and tweet things related to the industry. Create and connect with a network on LinkedIn and write blog entries others will find interesting. This comes from Chapter 9 about selling when there is no deal on the table. Create a brand for yourself to reinforce that you are all-in with what you are doing. Your customers can see what you are doing and it will expose you to more information to use when selling to them.

Colleagues

By throwing everyone I encountered in sales into the same basket of fake relationships, I am neglecting those that I really did care about and who cared about me. These are people that I am still friends with long after we left the companies we worked at together. In some cases, I was friends with these people before we worked together, which gave the relationship a stronger foundation. But others I met while on the job did become true friends. This was because while we were working together we could break the boundaries that existed among everyone else I knew. Once I got close enough to someone we could get "real" and share the same challenges and pains we had working in sales or for the companies we were with.

This doesn't happen often and by the nature of this deeper relationship it can't happen with more than a few people. If it did, the whole system would fall apart. But it's important to have one or two of these friendships so you can confide in someone. You are going to need to blow off steam with what you are experiencing and that trusted friend will be critical for that. It can help you express your feelings without holding them in until you explode. If you are joining a new company where you don't know anyone, it will take time to identify who that person might be. The catch-22 is that you need to be honest to find that person when that very honesty can expose you.

The relationships you have within sales is the best example of the pain with pleasure tradeoff that exists within the profession. On the pleasure side, sales can be fun. There will be a lot of socializing and meeting of people you will get to know and like. You will make friends and learn a lot from others. But on the other side you will encounter a lot of people you otherwise do not care about or like, but will be forced to interact with. It's the nature of the business. It's the nature of life.

Chapter 12: Ethics

You have to be trusted by the people that you lie to
So that when they turn their backs on you,
You'll get the chance to put the knife in

-Lyrics from *Dogs,* by Pink Floyd

In many of the stories from this book, and from others that were not published, I had the opportunity to compromise my morals to win the sale. Going into sales, I didn't realize how often I would have that option and how often I would take it. It was these actions that made me ask myself who I was and what kind of character I was building. I didn't like the answer.

That person on more than one occasion stretched the truth, embellished, lied, cheated, stole, and acted in other detrimental ways to make a sale. It's not that I didn't value my morals, it just became a natural part of those jobs, and eventually of my character, to lose sight of them. I also felt like what I was selling was doing more harm than good for society. This went as far back as my time selling textbooks when I thought every time I won, the students that had to pay a high cost for the books had lost. There was no one on the other end of that transaction who I thought was really benefiting from what I was doing. This happened everywhere I worked.

I spent a year working for Colloquy, a company owned by Kaplan Education. Kaplan has an extensive list of violations and lawsuits against them for aggressive recruiting tactics, subpar online programs, and dismal graduation rates. I worked for Blackboard, a company with a Learning Management System that dominates the market. Yet I mostly heard apologies from people because of how much they disliked their technology. This was my feeling at all the companies I worked for within higher education. It was all a business where students were viewed as "units" and a university was only as valuable as how much money they could spend. I was selling a product that wasn't doing anything to help anyone other than myself and a large corporation. My time with Thermal-Chem was the only honest sale I made where I was really helping a business.

What is unethical?

In sales, it's often not clear as to what is unethical because what I deem as such you might think is perfectly okay. An example of the subjectivity of what is unethical comes from the first story I told in Chapter 7 about wowing my customers. The committee was nearing a decision between my product and the incumbent competitor. A week before the final vote, they took an informal vote where my product lost easily. Someone from the committee I was close to told me about the vote but asked me not to approach anyone with that information because she was not supposed to share it.

Would you sit around for that week and let the final vote happen to respect what the person asked you to do or would you make a final push to try to salvage the deal? I was 24 and my sales career was just starting. The sale was an enormous one that would make me a lot of money and make a name for myself in the company. I chose to go to the committee members in the final days and aggressively sold my product one last time – something I would not have done if I didn't have the info about the informal vote since I felt I had already done everything I could to sell my product.

In the process, I met with one of the Advocates (remember this role from Chapter 5?) who became so compelled by my pitch that he emailed everyone the night before the final vote to say they had to choose my product. I also let it slip out that I knew about the informal vote. I won in a stunning comeback but my confidant found out I had shared the info she gave me. She felt betrayed and asked me not to work with her anymore in the future. We were close until that point. We had many fun conversations in her office and lunches of fried pickles and I sacrificed the relationship to make the sale. I wish it hadn't turned out that way but given the choice of her friendship or the sale it was obvious to me what to choose.

I traded a friend's trust for what I wanted. This is the gray area. Technically I didn't lie. I didn't promise her I wouldn't tell anyone. There was no rule saying I could not and maybe her friendship didn't mean anything to me. It's purely a question of what do I deem as being improper and what am I willing to live with. I gave up my integrity by trading my trust for a sale. I'm not proud of my actions but it's always easier to realize this when looking back. I wish I hadn't put myself in the position where it came to that, but these situations are inevitable in sales. But what you think is what you want will catch up to you when you realize later how wrong it was. Especially when actions like this lead you to use people as a means to an end.

Profit, profit, profit

Sales is a morally difficult field to work in because you're selling things for companies that demand the sale be made above anything else. Your livelihood is based on what they want, even if it conflicts with what you want. When money is the motivation behind a decision, those decisions can be based on emotion and bias towards your self-interest and the interests of the company. They are not based on what is best for your customer, yourself, and society at large. In 2009, a car crash killed a family of four in a Lexus when the accelerator was stuck due to defective floor mats. A month before that, executives from the company boasted of having negotiated a $100 million savings from their recall efforts of those mats. General Motors did the same thing with their ignition switch recall which lead to at least 13 deaths. When bonus checks are on the line and shareholders lurk around the corner, morals can get tossed aside.

I did this myself in the story from Chapter 2 with the bookstore that placed the same order three times by mistake. I knew it was a mistake but decided not to do anything when I could have prevented it. As a company, we were measured on gross sales so even when the store returned the unused books I would get full credit. But the bookstore got saddled with all the fees to return them. I made the decision so I could make money and figured my manager and everyone else would have wanted me to do the same.

Another example of when I had to overlook what I knew was right to make a sale followed the 2004 U.S. elections in November. The publisher I was with released "Election Update" versions of their American government books. The books were identical to the previous editions except they reflected the elections that just took place and had other minor changes. The company wanted the sales team to go to professors using the current editions and get them to switch to the Election Update for the spring semester. This was a bold move because professors rarely change an intro level book mid-year since it leaves little time to change their syllabus. They also don't do it so students taking the course in the fall can sell the book back to the bookstore who can resell it to students taking it in the spring semester to save them money. It's even more rare that they switch when a book changes so little from the previous version.

Nevertheless, with the company mandating we push the new edition, I went to my customers and made the pitch. I told them the book covered the changes in Congress and heated election between George W. Bush and John Kerry. I told them the book could include great new technology at no cost if they just asked the bookstore to ensure only the new edition be ordered. Through my pressure, most of them followed through. This was bad for the students who had to pay more money, bad for the bookstore who had to deal with the backlash from those students, and bad for the professor who had to update their syllabus to reflect the changes (and face backlash from students and the bookstore). The adoption of the new edition was good for one side: the company and myself.

You could blame the professor. They could have told me to get lost. They could have supplemented the current book with a few articles about the election. You could also blame the bookstore for not selling the professor on staying with the current edition as much as I did to switch. You could even blame the students for not refusing to buy the new book.

Again, what I did wasn't illegal. I didn't coerce anyone to use the new book. I just used my skills and charm to get what I wanted. Was it wrong to do this? It could be argued. The problem is that *I* knew what I was doing was wrong. I remember laughing with a colleague about how ridiculous the new edition was. I remember feeling ashamed when one professor showed me how 90% of both books were the same. I knew what I was selling and doing was fraught with dishonesty. Is this really what I wanted? I revere books and there I was selling a book I knew to be a complete sham. Looking back on it, it's hard to think I didn't revolt against it. But I chose not to because I knew I would make money and to keep the company profitable.

And what is the cost of this growth? I recall a time when a sales rep won an award and in her address to the sales team talked about how on many days her lunch consisted of coffee and a pack of certs, and everyone cheered. It was celebrated as a good thing that someone risked their physical well-being to make more sales. This way of always focusing on the bottom line also extends to mental well-being when the thought is always on the future and next quarter or year being the biggest and best ever.

What I got

I have an extensive list of other examples that are similar to situations other salespeople will be in. You'll have to make those decisions about what is right when they come to you. In return, you will get to work your own hours, and fewer hours than your non-sales colleagues. You'll likely work from home and get to spend a lot of days in sweatpants watching TV and running errands whenever you want. You will rarely run the rat race and sit in traffic for hours. You'll travel to fun locations, have an expense account, and meet a ton of great people. By 32 I had a nice bank account, a healthy 401k, a condo in downtown Austin, and a BMW. But none of these things I'd put on my top 10 list of what matters most in life.

It was an interesting trade of morals and integrity for money and self-glorification. But it wasn't always mutually exclusive. By making good money you can share it with others who need it. By having more time, you can give it to others through volunteering. By crafting your verbal and written skills, you can offer perspective to others. As corrupt as sales can make a person, it can also provide resources and skills to help a person be a functioning member of society, one who does a lot of good.

But even with the good that comes with it, you can still find yourself in a state of tension from holding two conflicting ideals at the same time. You might find the cognitive dissonance too much to bear. It's like watching the NFL knowing you'd never allow your son to start playing football so it's not him who's getting concussions. There might be a great result from what you are doing, but the ends don't always justify the means. You may have no problem selling a product you don't particularly like or care about as long as you get your commission. If you are lying to yourself, however, you can only do it for so long until you can no longer ignore it. But hopefully you'll be one of the smart ones and sell something you love because once you are, you're not in sales anymore.

The cognitive dissonance I faced was profiting off a higher education system that was and continues to be broken. I was working with college presidents and bloated bureaucracies of vice presidents in their jobs 10, 20, sometimes 30 years making huge salaries while presiding over dismal graduation rates. I watched in awe as the country accumulated a $1.3 trillion student loan bubble capable of bursting at any time and spreading havoc to the economy. I saw first-hand all the reasons so many universities were broken and I wanted to tear them apart and build them back up in a better way. But instead of being part of the solution or no part at all, I was part of the problem in helping to perpetuate the mess.

The people involved in selling these types of products are not bad. The editors, marketers, managers, sales people, and others with companies like this are good people. It's like the U.S. political system. The individual senators and congressmen that act in the interests of corporations over the people are not inherently bad. Many of them I'm sure, are just like you and me. The problem is that the system is corrupt. We are all operating under pressures that demand we act to keep these institutions strong, not ourselves. We are all part of the same machine that wants us to go along to keep the system of money and power afloat.

To see what others have done in response to this, Google "stories of people who left high paying sales jobs" and read countless stories of people leaving high paying jobs to do everything from backpacking around the world to starting their own company to living a healthier life and starting a family. These people realized life is more about making money.

It's not sales, it's me

But sales doesn't have to be like this for you. In fact, you are probably selling right now but maybe in a more authentic way. There's a popular sales book titled, *Everyone's in Sales,* by Todd Cohen. His main point is that no matter what you do, you are a salesperson. He reframes the word sales as communication. If you're a doctor, then you are a salesperson because you are trying to communicate to a patient why they should have surgery. If you're an artist, you're in sales because you are communicating your vision to lead to selling a painting. A mother is a salesperson because they are trying to communicate to their child why they should eat all their vegetables. As Charley from *Death of a Salesman* says, "The only thing you got in this world is what you can sell. And the funny thing is that you're a salesman, and you don't know that."

But to me, a Floor Coatings Representative for Thermal-Chem, a Course Materials Consultant for Wiley Education, and an Account Executive for Salesforce are all salesmen. In these cases, this is what I was and I was in the business of sales. The other examples of communicating are just humans working with other humans to help them as they go about their normal day-to-day actions. The difference between being in sales and being in life is whether your heart is really into whatever it is you are doing. And I can say for sure my heart has rarely been in any sales job I've done.

Have some fun

I want to take some time to remind you that while you are working in sales, make sure you have some fun along the way. If you don't then there really is no point. I can't deny that sales is fun. I've had amazing times during my career and feel so grateful for all my experiences. I've traveled on someone else's dime to great cities all over the country. While there, I stayed in 5-star hotels, eaten in fancy restaurants, and explored the nightlife. If this is the life you want, then sales has it for you.

When it comes to having fun, be careful. Addiction is common among salespeople. The Substance Abuse and Mental Health Services Administration puts the rate of drug and alcohol use in the field at 9.6%, which is higher than most professions. Based on what I saw, this number might be a huge underestimation. There are many factors that contribute to this, including the stress of needing to make sales, the constant travel and time away from home, and the inherent socializing and the pressure to fit in. If you already have an addiction or are prone to addictive behavior, understand that sales can exacerbate this through the nature of the work.

If you think you have an addiction or addictive behavior that is negatively affecting your life, don't be afraid to seek help. A therapist can be a big help as can a number of different recovery groups. One great resource that's based on cognitive science and the belief that you have the power to take control of your life and retrain yourself to make healthier choices is Self-Management and Recovery Training. You can learn more about SMART at www.SMARTrecovery.org.

Afterword: Find a Life to Love

You will serve an institution. You will serve, serve, serve…a much better idea would be to insist on the dignity of human beings.

-Terence McKenna

So there it is, everything I can tell you from my 15 years in sales. It's been an amazing journey. I've learned so much and although the way I was selling is not something I am entirely proud of, it has led me to a wonderful place where I love life more than ever and couldn't be more excited for the next phase. I hope you enjoyed this book as much as I did writing it, and that you learned a lot of things that can help you in your sales career, and more importantly, in life in general.

If I can leave you with any one final lesson, it's that whatever you do in your life as a profession, make sure you enjoy it and you're good at it. Those are the only two metrics to know if it's right for you. That may sound simple, but if it were, why did a 2017 survey from Gallup show that 67% of Americans are either unenthusiastic about, or downright hate, their job? I know I was in that majority for a while and perhaps you need to go on that road too in some way to eventually find what you want. If you do, make sure you learn from your mistakes. Life is an evolution and where we are today is not where we will be tomorrow, next week, next month, and beyond. But the sooner you find what you love, the sooner you will be living a life where you are truly happy. To get there, I encourage you to be honest with yourself, and don't hold back from following your truth.

About Atmosphere Press

Atmosphere Press is an independent full-service publisher for books in genres ranging from non-fiction to fiction to poetry, with a special emphasis on being an author-friendly approach to the often-brutal challenges of getting a book into the world. Learn more about what we do at Atmosphere's website, atmospherepress.com.

We encourage you to check out some of Atmosphere's latest releases, which are available at Amazon.com, BarnesandNoble.com, and via order from your local bookstore:

Rescripting the Workplace, nonfiction by Pam Boyd

Ghost Sentence, poems by Mary Flanagan

Bello the Cello, a children's book by Dennis Mathew

That Beautiful Season, a novel by Sandra Fox Murphy

What I Cannot Abandon, poems by William Guest

Such a Nice Girl, a novel by Carol St. John

All the Dead Are Holy, poems by Larry Levy

Surviving Mother, a novella by Gwen Head

Winter Park, a novel by Graham Guest

About Rashad Daoudi

Rashad Daoudi worked in sales for over 15 years at eight different companies, including Pearson Education, McGraw-Hill, and Salesforce. A Cleveland, OH native who graduated from Ohio University in 2002, Rashad ended his sales career in 2017 to publish *How Not to Sell* and to start Project Rashad, LLC, a project management and quality assurance company. He currently lives in Austin, TX. You can follow him at www.HowNotToSell.com.